D1649056

WE LOVED IT ALL

WE LOVED IT ALL

a memory of life

Lydia Millet

W. W. NORTON & COMPANY
Independent Publishers Since 1923

For information about permission to reproduce selections from this book, write to
Permissions, W. W. Norton & Company, Inc., 500 Fifth Avenue, New York, NY 10110

For information about special discounts for bulk purchases, please contact
W. W. Norton Special Sales at specialsales@wwnorton.com or 800-233-4830

Manufacturing by Lakeside Book Company
Book design by Anna Oler

ISBN 978-1-324-07365-9

W. W. Norton & Company, Inc., 500 Fifth Avenue, New York, N.Y. 10110
www.wwnorton.com

W. W. Norton & Company Ltd., 15 Carlisle Street, London W1D 3BS

1 2 3 4 5 6 7 8 9 0

CONTENTS

WHEN THE PERFECT COMES

1

IN THE BEGINNING we gave names to every creature that we found—the creeping things, the swimming things, the ones that walked and climbed and flew.

We gave them names, some say, so we might better know them.

Home was a garden, then—a garden in the wild. Green forests stretched up the feet of mountains, and clear rivers ran from ice-blue glaciers to the sea. Endless grasses on prairies rippled like water in the wind, and in the deserts a hot breeze blew the sands into dunes, silently shifting across the deep rock.

The creatures we named roamed through the woods and fields and oceans in abundance. More animals than you could ever imagine.

We were animals too. And like the others felt no embarrassment, seeing no need to cover our bodies.

At first we were safe in the garden, which was an earthly paradise. We were permitted to eat the fruit of every tree that grew in it, as the story goes, with one exception: the fruit of the tree of knowing good from evil.

Because even paradise has rules.

And if we'd stopped there, before we reached for that fruit at the start of it all—showing no curiosity, seeking no knowledge, and content in our innocence and ignorance—we might have been allowed to stay in that beautiful garden.

Live in the beginning forever.

BETWEEN THE END of my childhood and the moment I had a child of my own, there stretched a span of time like the arc of a thrown ball.

From the point when my young hand let loose the ball until my older hand caught it, I followed its curve through the air and felt impervious. It was easy to be independent and defiant. Even cold. Nothing held me captive, and if any friction slowed me down it was only the icy burn of atmosphere.

I see it now, though I didn't see it then. It was the freedom of having nothing to risk but myself.

When you turn into a mother you lose the power of coldness. Lose it for good, as it happens. You never get it back.

Once you have children, you know they can be hurt or even killed. Then you're humbled forever. A beggar at the mercy of the world.

CHILDLESS ADULTS ARE on the rise, in most industrialized countries, and birth rates are falling—a trend that correlates with women's education and access to family planning. Only a few years ago, the percentage of people who chose never to have children was in the low single digits; now it's well into the doubles. Both women and men are deciding more often to have fewer or no children. Yet across the globe our kind proliferates, pressing itself hard and fast over the land, replacing forests and wetlands with crops and pasture, wildlife with livestock, variety with sameness.

Myself, though I worry about our numbers, I chose to have children partly from curiosity—a curiosity tinged with selfishness. In defiance of reason, possibly.

These motivations are hardly uncommon. And I don't regret having children. If I did I wouldn't brag about it, but the truth is that I never have and never will.

Still, I recall my life before. How it was marked by a looseness of time and movement.

And an availability to risk.

AFTER MY FIRST baby was born, in the dual terrain of protectiveness and vulnerability new parents navigate, I realized that to be a decent mother and still get my work done I'd have to keep to a regimented schedule.

I'd have to organize my days. Caregiving tasks, my day job, my own writing, and after the sun set, and the baby was tucked into bed, a couple of hours of leisure like a long exhalation. Those hours were a velvet twilight—my charge was safely asleep, while I was still awake and could relax my vigilance.

The child, a daughter, was sustained. Four years later another baby arrived, a son. Likewise sustained. I cared for them and even doted on them, delighted by their small forms. Bought them food and made sure it was healthy, though—full disclosure—its wholesomeness would decline over the years. As I became more captive to their wills. And also lazier.

When they were little I dressed them and kept them clean. Took them to the doctor at the intervals officially designated for such visits. She gave them shots and printed out graphs showing how their weight and height compared to the weight and height of other children.

For many years, I read to them almost every night. At work, projects were duly undertaken and completed.

Only routine made those completions possible.

But now and then I'd be gripped by a sudden, frightened conviction that I should drop my regular habits. With their pretense of normalcy. That I should have dropped them long ago.

Because the indications are very strong that we don't live in normal times. If there have ever been normal times, even if there's a sliding scale or a spectrum, our own are an outlier.

And sometimes it seems clear to me that the normalcy most of us cling to so stubbornly—assuming it like a cloak against the changing weather—is also a paralysis. A blithe insistence on the continuity of daily life. It must go on, it can't go on, it goes on.

Fleetingly, then, I'm taken back to moments when I was young and alone. Between one second and the next I'd be swept up, usually by music but sometimes by a book, in a tremor of exultation I couldn't describe: a vibrant, impossible hope.

A radiance of being. Shivering, barely balanced, on a rim of despair. After the moment faded, I'd feel stricken. Touched by an unseen hand, then left.

The rapture passed, and in its wake was only the familiar flatness of the present.

HOW TO RECAPTURE the rush of possibility that surpasses description? The thrill of an imaginary flight?

To give ourselves over to that rush—to the giddy euphoria of displacement from the normal and regular—some choose religion, some choose drugs, some choose a constant stream of new stimuli or the rigor of exercise. Our escape takes many forms, but always occurs within the structure of a story: even when we don't know what we're escaping from, we know we need something or somewhere to escape *to*. Moving forward and forward again into the shape of a personal future, we exist in a narrative of aspiration—a hopeful arc of awakening and victory that we receive from the mythmakers of our culture.

And when the hollowness or hardness of our work presses us down, the pale repetition of our days, we cling to that fictional arc of triumph. If our real life fails again and again to uplift us, we still have a story of that life to believe in. A story of infinite potential.

Maybe it's the dullness and stress of labor from which we need an escape; maybe it's failures with family or friends. Or maybe it's less personal—maybe the escape is from a larger landscape, from the omnipresent evidence of social and natural disintegration that reaches our senses from the streets and media. Maybe it's an intuition of ongoing trauma to the world.

To many of us, what can be done in place of business as usual remains unknown. Where drugs or religion or dissent are out of reach, we go to homier and handier vices: alcohol and food and the catharsis of entertainment and goods-buying. Minor and pettier disruptions that roll more neatly into the course of daily events but, like narcotics, allow us to avoid a painful confrontation with the conditions of the real.

Like many of us, I register a sense of shame at my inertia.

And keep on going as before.

IT PASSES SO QUICKLY, doesn't it? It seems like just yesterday that they were babies! One moment they were tiny, and then—They were in kindergarten, and now she's driving. Look at that little guy—well no, he's not exactly little anymore, but you know what I mean. Last time I saw him he was wearing diapers, clinging to your leg. And now he's off to college.

These are the things the parents say to each other. *It passes so fast, it seems like yesterday that . . .* clichés of recognition that feel necessary, rather than trite, because they touch against a genuine puzzlement—a confusing encounter with change over time. Grapple with the tension between closeness and detachment, always uncertain and never resolved.

To the child, a parent has a sort of solidity. Whether the mother or father is kind or punitive, steady or stumbling, affectionate or distant, she or he remains a figure that changes little over the period of their mutual dependency, in voice and shape and habit—at least compared to the child. The child grows up to meet the parent, who meanwhile dwindles, in her sight, from a giant to a peer.

To a parent the child is a being in metamorphosis, in a state of constant becoming and unbecoming. A child is no longer a baby, no longer a toddler, no longer a small child . . . no longer, apparently, a child at all.

But still and always *the* child.

As the parent shrinks, the child grows larger and more powerful. And when a certain parity is reached—a parity agreed upon by social convention and physical age, often between eighteen and twenty-one—the child is set free.

So the task of any parent is paradoxical: a devotional intimacy aimed at inevitable separation. A long, dedicated service of gifting and appease-ment, care and adoration that's bound to end in the absence of its idol.

A child is a god who goes away.

WHEN WE'RE SMALL we're enveloped in the images and lore of other creatures. Pets, barnyard favorites, and then the wild kind, so fabulous they might have been invented purely for our delight.

Some have golden, spotted necks so impossibly long that their heads seem to float above the trees. Or dexterous, gray, tubular noses that act like arms and can trumpet loud sounds and spray fountains of water. Some are covered in lustrous feathers, silver scales, or elaborate segments of armored plates.

Some look like translucent bells, floating in water and trailing a mass of curling ribbons. Some have heavy laceworks of antlers sitting on their brows or great maws like sieves that seem to swallow the ocean. Some have so many legs we can't count them. Or no legs at all.

The stuff of fantasy and dreams.

Their names teach us the alphabet—introduce us to language itself. A is for alligator. C is for cat.

We imitate the sounds they make: Cats go meow. Cows go moo. We wear their pictures on our clothes, clutch soft ones to our chests when we lie down. Play with figures cast in their shapes, ride on them in play-grounds and carousels. Small replicas circle our heads in mobiles, deco-rate our sheets and pillowcases. Talking and singing versions are the stars of our stories, in shows and video games and books.

Children know and define themselves, and other people, by the attri-butes of beasts. Their looks and movements and behaviors, the charac-teristics we ascribe to them, come also to describe our own. We can be proud as a peacock, mean as a snake. Get squirrelly or monkey around. Be a chicken.

The other animals are both real and metaphor: they're everywhere.

This saturation ends in the teenage years, as children surrender their imaginary play for structured activities with quantifiable outcomes—grades and scores, winners and losers—that teach them to achieve and struggle to prevail. Now the leisure prescribed to them is guided competition: play disguised as contests, then contests disguised as play. The animals become relics of a frivolous time. Back when the future did not loom, when fantasy reigned in the sprawling gardens of a long and formless summer.

Thus the wild creatures cease to adorn our children's clothes, outside the odd ironic unicorn-with-rainbow T-shirt or stylized team mascot on a uniform. We-the-parents are co-conspirators in this gesture of relegation, divesting bedrooms of old animal companions. Shoving them into the backs of closets, giving them away to younger kids, stuffing them into Goodwill bins.

Where they once were, the children put up posters of people they admire. Models of excellence or glamour: actors, musicians, athletes. Celebrities and leaders.

We thank the other animals for their service—some with a pang, some without so much as a backward glance—and they bow out into the wings.

We do away with childish things, for it's time to set our sights on people.

So the children come to see themselves as lone individuals in training for the marketplace. Far from the community of the natural world, which seems to lie beyond and outside the real and practical arena.

Our economy, like our life support, is derived from nature in its entirety—but even so those young adults are taught that nature is a separate domain. That its collective is a distant irrelevance: they need to carry a torch of competition and specialization into the urban and manufactured spaces, the battlefield of earning. Bend the field to their will and make it furnish them with riches.

Growing up is an abandonment of the beasts.

And in that abandonment our journey mirrors the arc of our culture's history, which has also turned its face away from other animals. As time went on.

AS A PARENT, I have to picture my children grown old. This ideation is a vicious punishment for raising young—the realization that our children, if they're lucky enough to survive that long, will, in the passing of time, become decrepit like us.

No longer beautiful, as we once knew them to be. No longer strong, no longer shining. Hobbled by infirmity. Even more fragile and defenseless than when they were small.

For a parent, the probability that you won't be around to witness their aging and dying—whose reality itself, mostly, you shun—is a partial comfort.

And even that meager solace is compromised: You won't be around to see their decline, true. But you also won't be around to protect them.

2

THE OTHER ANIMALS don't vanish from our lives as we grow up: they stick around, working in sales.

They persist as front men for commodities. When we're little, animated tigers, birds, and rabbits offer us sweet cereals and chocolate milk while we watch cartoons; smiling cows adorn the labels of cheese. But they also march along the walls of our classrooms with letters beside them or starred in our picture books and movies.

Now the sales jobs seem to be their main gig. They show up as hood ornaments on cars, tell us about the charms of cigarettes and alcohol, clothing and shoes and insurance policies. Adorn military hardware and medals and insignia. Some are emblazoned on rippling flags, representing states or nations.

In their role as logos and spokespersons they have broad appeal: I've known a certain witty gecko with a Cockney accent for most of my adult life. I'm aware the impish gecko is playing on my sensibilities, but I haven't stopped liking him.

Much is lost when the animals are turned into brand ambassadors: their reduction takes a toll on our imaginations. In the sales racket their charisma and distinctness are no longer their own but stand in for human qualities or corporate prestige. The jaguar on a car is a proxy for the driver who's purchased it, sleek and predatory. The alligator on polo shirts is a symbol of the wealth and country-club values of their wearers.

We aren't stupid: we always knew tigers don't eat breakfast foods made from corn. We always understood that lizards don't have a use for car insurance policies. Yet as the casual currency of their images is spent and respent and finally devalued, the intimacy we once shared with the beasts, along with the awe we felt at the splendor of their differences, begins to fade.

They become cheapened versions of themselves, tricked out to sell us swag—graphics before beings. Demeaning those they impersonate. Objectified and servile.

I FEAR THAT MY CHILDREN, one day—mine and the children of others—will be forced to endure the vanishing of much more than we ever did. Of a far greater legion.

I fear the despair of a helpless witnessing.

Who has already gone? Do we still know their names?

Who is going today?

And who will be going tomorrow?

OF THE ONES who've disappeared most recently, we have some video and audio. Of the ones that went soon before them, like the Tasmanian tiger, we have black-and-white photographs and a handful of films a few seconds long. In the spliced-together footage, a stripey-backed thylacine, possibly the last, paces in a cage and jumps at the mesh—we see the brief flash of a metal tag around her neck.

We see her lie down in a patch of sun, sniff the air with her pointed snout, and then rest her chin on her paws to sleep.

TASMANIAN TIGERS, ALSO called thylacines, were carnivorous marsupials that lived in mainland Australia, the southern island of Tasmania, and New Guinea. They looked more like dogs than tigers—their closest living relatives are Tasmanian devils and numbats, both endangered now.

The last thylacine of them all, often incorrectly referred to as "Benjamin," was given that name posthumously by a man who claimed to have been a keeper at the Hobart Zoo but whose claims were probably spurious. The zoo had declined, and its animals were being neglected—a decline that was due in large part, as Robert Paddle documented in *The Last Tasmanian Tiger*, to sexism among humans: the only person willing and able to take care of it—the daughter of a curator, who struggled valiantly to take over his duties after he died—was denied the funds and power to do so by the zoo's trustees, who refused to support her efforts on the basis that she was a woman.

The last thylacine was a female who died in 1936, when she was locked out of the warm part of her enclosure overnight in a cold snap and froze.

BEFORE THE TECHNOLOGIES of recording existed, we made drawings or paintings of the last animals—dodos, say, or great auks.

Great auks were the last species in the now-extinct genus *Pinguinus*: modern penguins were named for their resemblance to auks. These were large, flightless birds that coexisted with Neanderthals, who ate them more than a hundred thousand years ago.

The Beothuks, a long-extinct culture in what's now called Newfoundland, made pudding from their eggs.

The legend of the great auk's obliteration goes like this: The final two confirmed birds were killed in 1844 on a rocky island off the coast of Iceland, where they were found incubating an egg by three men charged with the task of gathering specimens for a merchant. To be shipped off to a collector.

"It was incredible, they were just sitting there looking quite dignified," said one of the men, by the name of Ketill Ketilsson, in an interview with the English naturalists John Wolley and Alfred Newton. (Wolley was a

specimen collector himself and would go on to make a forensic expedi-
tion to Iceland and write books about the demise of the "garefowl.")

Despite this dignity, two of the men strangled the nesting pair, and a
third smashed their egg under his boot.

Those three men were the last auk-killers, it would seem. But most of
the work of auk extinction had been done in Newfoundland during the
century before.

DIORAMAS HAVE BEEN built to evoke the presence of the vanished
ones, some by natural history museums and others by lone enthusiasts.
I took my children to see some of these museum landscapes when they
were little, and recently watched a video of one—a labor of love by a man
named Martin Bright of Queensland, Australia, now deceased—that was
set to music and beautifully re-created a scene of a flock of passenger
pigeons in the wild.

Watching a video of that diorama, I had tears in my eyes. A world of
creatures I'd never seen. Full of tiny, painstaking simulations of birds in
flight who would never fly again.

Yet still, as I write this, we haven't witnessed the extinction of any
of the animals that were the fast friends of our early childhoods. There
remain, in the vanishing wild, polar bears stalking their prey in the Far
North. Even as their ice melts and they starve or drown. Tigers in the jungles and steppes, lions in the savannas, elephants and blue whales, giant
pandas and kangaroos.

Many of these are in danger. And it may be that species like polar
bears, despite the melting sea ice that threatens them so clearly, are not
the first to fall.

Possibly, too, the presence of captive animals in zoos will allow us to
believe, after their wild populations have winked out, that the species
still exist.

I've been comforted, in the past, by the idea that zoos are a sort of safe
house—a treasure trove of creatures much like Noah's Ark. That despite

the many flaws of zoos, despite their history and present of enforced captivity, they guard a legacy of being. Where animals are protected from the threat of extinction—from the ravages of a risky, free-roaming existence subject to human pressures, aggression, and mischief.

But when the last wild population of a species disappears, the designs and methods of its eating and mating, and the social systems to which its zoo-dwelling, captive remnants once belonged, are no longer available for them to return to.

Their *culture*—a word some don't like to use for the lifeways of other animals, but which nonetheless describes the intricate, often intangible web of individual and group behaviors all complex beings rely on to survive—can no longer be passed down to them in the homes they used to have. They persist as bodies on the stages of their captivity. They breathe, eat, sleep, and may possibly be persuaded to reproduce. But many may be condemned, absent a greater family beyond the walls, to a solitary entombment.

I wonder whether the disappearance of the first of our childhood companions will shock us as lower-profile disappearances have not. Or whether the day will come when animals like elephants and polar bears become, to our grandchildren or their children, figures as distant as the dinosaurs are to my son Silas now—plastic simulacra they can play with sitting cross-legged on the floor. Which no longer have any living referents in the world beyond their playrooms.

I wonder if, before that day comes, a jarring disturbance caused by the permanent loss of a friend from youth will allow us to feel with greater urgency the weight and fear of absence.

PASSENGER PIGEONS ARE a notorious extinction, in part because of their onetime plenitude. In the nineteenth century, they may have been the most numerous birds anywhere.

Flocks of millions darkened the skies over American cities. Blotting out the sun, said the naturalist and writer Aldo Leopold. Their survival strategies hinged on that very abundance: alighting in clouds that reached to the horizon to eat their preferred acorns and beechnuts, they depended on sheer numbers to survive predation. At nesting time, they'd take over whole forests.

When they were hunted into scarcity for food—not only with guns but in coordinated campaigns of mass tree-burnings, asphyxiations with sulfur, and frenetic attacks with pitchforks and rakes—the smaller remaining populations crashed.

Simon Pokagon, a leader in the Potawatomi tribe who'd watched and admired the passengers since he was a boy, witnessed the wasteful scorched-earth tactics used by the colonists to kill them. He wrote about it, wondering what punishment would be visited upon whites "who have so wantonly butchered and driven from our forests these wild pigeons, the most beautiful flowers of the animal creation of North America."

The slaughter of the passengers was enacted on a monumental scale, like the slaughter of the American bison and pronghorns and wolves, but unlike those other mass killings, it finished without a single survivor—commercial and amateur killers alike hunted the pigeons voraciously until every one of them was gone.

And some three billion birds were turned into zero.

THE TERM *ENDLING* came, in the 1990s, to refer to an animal that is the last one of its kind.

Some endlings have been celebrities of solitude, with names and faces that are widely known. They've had human keepers to feed them and try to breed them and received a measure of public attention for their plight—if only in retrospect.

The last Pinta Island tortoise, Lonesome George, lived for more than forty years after the rest of his kind were driven to extinction by an introduced population of goats gone feral. He was probably a century old when he died of cardiac arrest in 2012.

There had been many attempts to mate him with other subspecies of

Galápagos tortoise, in hopes that a hybrid might be produced, allowing his genotype to live on. But unlike his tortoise colleague Diego, who mated avidly and publicly, George was a reluctant mater. Near the end of his life he finally, obligingly mated, but none of the resulting eggs were viable.

His preserved and mounted body is on display in the Galápagos, at the Charles Darwin Research Station.

The passenger pigeon named Martha was believed to be twenty-nine years old when she died in the Cincinnati Zoo in 1914. She'd never laid an egg that hatched and suffered from a palsy that made her tremble.

Celia the ibex died in 2000, her skull crushed by a falling branch. A clone created from her skin samples, implanted into the egg of a domestic goat and carried to term by an ibex of another subspecies, was born in 2009 but died minutes after birth.

Rabb's fringe-limbed tree frogs disappeared when an endling called Toughie died in 2016. He'd lived there since 2005, when he was collected from a Panamanian cloud forest by biologists racing to rescue his species from the deadly chytrid fungus. Other Rabb's fringe-limbed tree frogs were gathered and shipped with him, including some tadpoles, but they soon perished in captivity.

According to those who took care of him at the Atlanta Botanical Garden, he didn't like to be touched, and when he wished to be put down, would pinch their hands.

In 2014, after nine years in the zoo, he called for the first time, with none of his kind remaining to hear him. Though he died two years later, the call was recorded and can still be heard.

The dusky seaside sparrows of Florida's Merritt Island, right next to Cape Canaveral, were small, ground-feeding wetland birds whose serious decline began with the spraying of DDT on their marshes in the 1940s. Roads were built, along with dikes to impound water, and the "duskies" had trouble feeding.

Then NASA flooded their habitat to reduce mosquitoes around the nearby Kennedy Space Center. In 1983 the four last pure dusky sparrows were taken to Disney World. They were all males, so crossbreeding efforts began.

But the birds were old, and the few hybrid chicks that hatched ended up dying not long after the breeding program shut down.

The final dusky, Orange Band, blind in one eye from an infection, infertile, extremely aged, and possibly suffering from gout, was found dead in his food bowl in the summer of 1987.

3

WHEN SHE WAS a preteen my daughter liked the kind of young adult books and films in which teenage couples gradually succumb to terminal cancer. Or waste away in mutual, frustrated pining from another hideous disease that, while killing them, also prevents them from ever touching. In one novel she particularly enjoyed, a mother backed over her baby in the family car and killed him because his sister, the protagonist sitting in the passenger seat, was the only one who could see the baby in the rearview mirror. Having a speech disability, however, she couldn't warn her mother in time.

Young adult stories aren't for the faint of heart—the territory of their melodrama often stretches far beyond what's deemed palatable in so-called literary novels. But Nola wasn't deterred.

Yet when it comes to the suffering of animals she's always said no. No to nature shows. Emphatically. No even to live-action movies where fictional animals die.

My son feels the same way.

Once I tried to have us watch a movie called *Warhorse* where, in an early scene, a horse was worked to death. As it fell to its knees, they both started crying and left the room.

It's different with animation, though—animated animals are allowed.

So when they were little we watched favorites from my childhood like *Animal Farm* and *Watership Down.*

I felt a chill when the pigs in *Animal Farm,* led by the cruel Stalinist pig Napoleon, rewrote the commandment *All animals are equal* to read: *All animals are equal, but some are more equal than others.*

I cried at the end of *Watership Down*—as the children smiled pityingly and reassured me—when Hazel, the patient and gentle leader of the rabbits, made lame in his youth by a bullet to the leg, grew elderly and quiet in the peace of the rolling hills.

And one day had to leave his dear family behind. No longer lame, he bounded in freedom across the sky with the black rabbit of Inlé. Who was also known as Death.

An old friend come to take away his burdens. And welcome him home at last.

THIS IS A TIDBIT I haven't dared to share with the children: in the coal mines of England, France, and Australia, late into the twentieth century, there were horses taken down into the mines as foals who stayed there till they died. Never saw the sun again, cropped the green grass, breathed fresh air, or walked beneath the sky.

"Pit ponies" was the endearing English name for these subterranean beasts of burden. They hauled great weights for their masters, pulling coal, and when they fell dead of exhaustion, their bodies were simply left to decay.

In fact the horses had replaced women and children in many of those mines: when it was publicized, after a mass drowning of twenty-six children in a single collapse in 1838, that small girls and boys were being worked underground, a new law was passed banning the use of those under ten. (Later the age was changed to thirteen.)

At the height of the pit ponies' deployment, there were some seventy thousand being worked in English mines alone.

As a class, they were championed by horse lovers and eventually released from service.

With the mechanization of labor, horses made a transition from work animals to useful companions. Now they occupy a curious space between livestock and pet—supplying us with neither meat nor dairy but still bearing us on their backs.

The last of the wild ones, Przewalski's horses, were reintroduced to Mongolia from a captive-bred population in 1992.

The second-to-last kind, a subspecies called the tarpan, disappeared in the early 1900s. The tarpan may have gone extinct in Russia in captivity in 1909, but some claim the captive animal that died that year was a hybrid or feral domesticated horse. The only illustration I can find of a tarpan drawn from life dates from 1841 and looks quite different from the alleged last animal in the Russian zoo: it features a curved brow and more tapered head.

All other horses sometimes referred to as "wild" are feral—domesticated horses that have been set free or escaped. Or those animals' descendants.

OUR EMPATHY RARELY EXTENDS to cattle and poultry: the very words *cattle* and *poultry* are a denial of empathy, transacting the living into the already-dead and already-food.

We distance ourselves with an armor of words even when we admit to animals' acute powers of perception or amiable characters. This was brought home to me as a kid by books such as *Charlotte's Web*, whose lessons in sympathy were taught again, repeatedly, to my own children by movies like *Babe*. Pigs have feelings, the books and the movies suggested. Possibly spiders can show love.

After childhood we rarely linger on the subject of, say, pigs' intelligence—we prefer to linger instead on the undeniable pleasures of bacon, ham, and pork.

Pigs and cows who're bred for slaughter by the hundreds of millions, and the 65 billion chickens killed and eaten every year, mostly pass their years crushed into cramped positions in soiled cages. Dairy cows have multiple babies taken from them so their milk can feed us instead. Many of these creatures spend their last moments in fear and pain.

On the wild side, though precise figures are harder to determine, about 40 percent of the fish that get scooped from the ocean every year—of a total catch of more than 100 million metric tons—are immediately discarded, dead or dying, as "bycatch." Hundreds of thousands of marine mammals, sea turtles, and seabirds are also accidentally killed by our fisheries each year—a fatality rate that will cause many species to vanish entirely.

Efforts to persuade our institutions and instruments of commerce to clear a space of respect for other lifeforms, whether in fishing or agriculture or trade, are routinely waved off as strident or hysterical. Such efforts are irritants to the market, for sure, but also threaten the grand permission we've given ourselves to use the bodies of other animals.

For most of us, to speak or even think of the masses of unfortunates is not the accepted custom.

As it is also not the custom to stand in the middle of a crowd emitting a slow, ululating wail.

AS PART OF ITS sweeping rollback of all forms of protective laws, the Trump administration relaxed slaughterhouse rules in 2019, increasing line speeds in hog slaughterhouses across the country. And decreasing the number of federal inspections of live animals required at those facilities.

One such inspector, in a statement submitted to a court in 2020 in support of retaining the stronger slaughterhouse rules, attested to the fact that their weakening would increase the animals' suffering.

It would also, she testified, increase fecal contamination and the incidence of diseased animals being sold to, and eaten by, the public. Along with more of their toenails, hair, and abscesses.

These were among the many gifts of deregulation.

SOME COWS ARE FISTULATED. This means a hole is cut in their sides and fitted with a plastic port, which they retain for life.

You can stick your gloved arm through the hole right into the cow's body—its rumen, where beneficial microorganisms can then be collected by your rummaging hand. These stomach bugs can help other, sick cows to heal.

At veterinary and agricultural schools, fistulated cows are fairly common. Proponents say it doesn't hurt, and that cows with windows cut into their bodies are perfectly happy.

However. They have yet to reveal their secret methods of measuring cow happiness.

4
—

TRY TO BE HAPPY, says the Declaration of Independence. And pop songs. And greeting cards. Even the media-friendly Dalai Lama, fourteenth of his name.

Happiness is the goal.

Myself, I want it for sure. Everyone does. It's good!

But then . . . what is it, exactly?

I *have* to know, I think. Of *course* I know. I can imagine how it feels, casting through the pleasant scenes that I recall.

One glowing day . . . an uplift out of nowhere, a sense of peace . . . a picnic, all of us laughing so hard we cried, people running down a grassy hill . . . or no.

They may have been scenes from movies, actually. Except the one about the laughter. And maybe the one about the peace.

But those things have their own names.

Sometimes, I realize, it's a label I put on a time after the time has passed, from the far side of a threshold. I didn't recognize it then, but we were happy.

Or casting forward into an aspiration. We'll be happy when . . . but *will* we? Or is there always a false summit, and once we stand on it, we see the other, higher peaks ahead? Crowned in mist?

In some watered-down versions of folk and fairy tales, happiness is a plateau. Once you reach it, it goes on and on. Happily ever after.

But that can't be right, can it? A plateau doesn't extend forever. After a while, it drops off in a cliff.

There's the prospect of pleasure, of course—the passing delights of the body and of the new. But by definition we can't have newness constantly. And most of us don't know how to translate delight into that lasting, possibly imaginary state someone once told us, and then kept telling us repeatedly, was out there.

Happiness is a wavering mirage that shimmers on the horizon, a promise of sudden deliverance that supports the passive attendance of our lives. Invites us to wait, wait, wait, for the perfect to manifest itself.

Descending like an angel from the clouds.

What we actually need may be something less vague and more attainable: an embrace of the real over a constantly deferred ideal, an engagement with the precious and finite time that's given us.

An exhilaration of presence. Not as simple as the affects *happy* and *sad*, but both and more.

And everything.

ALONG WITH THE happy ending, a shared feature of our most epic and lasting cultural myths is the dominance of a lone hero. Usually a version or projection of *us* or of *me*. The heroes have to be relatable, with admirable qualities we aspire to but also enough familiar foibles to render them "human" and allow them to serve as proxies for our flawed but still admirable selves.

What we follow are the arcs of a victorious self: a self that rises ascendant, against all odds, over hostile, misguided, or otherwise inferior others. For at least five years, as a child, Silas fought constant Nerf sword battles with an imaginary opponent—an invisible enemy in the living room or backyard. And this habit was not unique to him.

Transfixed by these striving monomyths of heroes as winners, which we watch and retell in countless iterations, we see ourselves as possible heroes and winners too. And lose sight of the fact that this plotline of competition and triumph is a highly specific invention, as purpose-built as a blender or bicycle. It tells us to seek to be *better than*: that being *better than* depends on a selfhood of striving, that striving translates to winning and winning translates to happiness.

The story of winning seems to serve our own wants, laden with punishments and rewards along the road, while the fact that those personal wants neatly serve the needs of the marketplace appears as a natural coincidence.

Even the smaller judgments we make about our doings—how a day or a conversation has gone, a work interaction or a snag in a relationship—are instantly embedded into the storyline of wins and losses, reinforcing or briefly undermining the shape and direction of that storyline's preexisting arc.

Immersed in the rapid conversion of happening and feeling into self-reflecting meaning, we tend to discard signposts and side streets that lead beyond the storyline's terrain. Passing over those features of the landscape that don't flow into the arc.

It's an arc we often describe unconsciously, through time, since many of us choose our stories of selfhood at some crucial juncture in youth and spend the rest of our lives chasing an afterimage. Straining to fit the new into a fading imprint of purpose and desire.

I remember the stories I used to tell myself about my life when I was a teenager and on into my twenties—I remember their romance and their shine. I will do this, I will be that. After defeat, I will gather myself and regroup. After a victory, I will build.

As I got older the stories became less epic and more like ensemble pieces: my role in them shifted, tilting away from the heroic. More and more I came to understand myself as a face in a crowd instead of a principal with top billing—a crowd made up of a thousand extras, each with their own arrows of private aspiration.

Still, my stories of myself are vestiges of childish fragments of make-believe. It's hard to relinquish a dream mythology of meaning and of relevance, to give up on the longing for a parent's praise. The surreptitious yearning to ascend out of the everyday.

Into the pantheon of the exceptional.

IN ELEMENTARY SCHOOL my daughter and son brought home the products of numerous arts-and-crafts projects.

Occasionally these were arresting to look at—I keep a relief map that my son made of the state of Arizona, where we live, displayed near my desk—but typically the arts and crafts were items whose poignancy was matched only by their lack of practical function.

Lopsided vessels fashioned out of clay, wood, glass, or melted polymer beads, too small to contain anything but paper clips or thumbtacks. Tissue-paper flowers in painted bottles or cans, masks made of Styrofoam plates with protruding pipe cleaners and loosely glued-on feathers or sequins they shed wherever they went. A plaster cactus in a pot, then two: for many years the children attended the same school, and the plaster cacti, probably meant to evoke our local saguaros, were canonical.

An object might secure its position on the shelves with a heartwarming inscription. *For my Mommy. Your the best from Sy.* Or *To Mama From Nola Age 5. I ♥ you Forever.*

I was a sucker for these, though I detected the guiding hand of a teacher in their fashioning. Had my daughter been inspired, all by herself, to write *Age 5*?

Sometimes I'd curse as I studied an inscription. *Damn!* I'd say through gritted teeth. *Can't throw* this *one away. Well, shit.*

It seemed the stream was unending. If you're a parent, you too must have faced the arts-and-crafts dilemma: if each item made by our children were dutifully revered, our living spaces would quickly be converted into garishly colored, decaying craft museums.

After a while, in our fairly small house, the children's artistic productivity took on a diabolical aspect.

But it also mirrored my own artistic productivity a bit too neatly—a discomfiting hint at the futility of all making, all constant offering-up of handmade creations, from sequined and misshapen cactus pots to symphonies or novels.

Each object, in its poignancy and imperfections, referred to the poignancy and imperfections of objects beyond itself. We *all* wish to be exceptional, the stream of efforts seemed to remind me—despite my children's indifference to their own creations, which as far as I could tell they usually viewed as the end result of a process of forced labor.

Still, extravagant praise might be lavished by an adult on a given cactus pot or painted-rock paperweight—I saw this with other parents as well as teachers. It seemed our child-rearing approach involved encouraging our progeny to see their every product as a work of brilliance.

We would be a nation of hundreds of millions of exceptions.

FOR YEARS I SPENT three afternoons a week in a warehouse studio about forty-five minutes' drive from our home, where Nola, starting when she was six, attended classes in aerial acrobatics and circus arts.

Periodically I'd look up from chasing Sy as he toddled around the margins of the room, barely avoiding cartwheeling preteens and novice jugglers. And catch my breath in alarm as Nola, hanging eighteen feet up in the air with only a swath of fabric wrapped around her ankles and torso, plummeted quickly toward the floor in rapid flips and rolls. Then came to rest with her head a couple of inches from the mat.

The studio space was used for various activities besides acrobatics and dance—drumming, martial arts, yoga. One wall was covered in artworks by adults, a motley assemblage of paintings and prints. A few bore modest price tags.

They included a large, tapestry-like hanging that combined picture with words. I gazed at the text many times but don't remember much about the image behind it—the outline of a woman, I faintly recall. Possibly holding an infant.

It bore the following legend: *I dream of a world where one day my child will turn to me and ask, "O Mother, what was war?"*

The tapestry fascinated me, in its good intentions and naïveté.

It seemed like a cautionary tale. For all artists.

THE ART OF STORY is the spirit of any culture but also its substance. Information that gets conveyed to us outside the linear excitement of narrative—in the recitation of facts, in scientific reporting, in drier coverage of events and policy and law—is taken up by our minds with disinterest. Or not at all.

Only story can bring it home.

Lifelines that guide us through the diffuse fog of existing, stories make sense of the complex and shifting miasma of perception. They're how the human brain organizes sensory data into consciousness, time and events into coherence. Personhood is built out of narrative units, without which the divisions between self and not-self would tend to dissolve.

Because stories are social, transmissible, and adaptable, our stories of ourselves are made up of those of others, which we mimic and re-form to suit our needs. Recent scholarship has also shown that stories are empathy-creators in the brain—something most filmgoers and filmmakers, readers and storytellers know well—partly through the synthesis of oxytocin, a love hormone or "moral molecule," as the researcher Paul Zak calls it.

And we tend to fix our attention, in fiction and nonfiction alike, on individual biography. Our most-read and most-watched stories tend to abandon the political and philosophical and cleave to the domain of selfhood, to the small circles of personal lives and the close-by interactions of a self with its intimates.

In the 1990s Robin Dunbar, a British anthropologist studying primates, proposed that the primate brain, including that of humans—specifically the neocortex—has developed with cognitive constraints on group size: it tends to embrace interaction with only a limited number of other individuals. This "Dunbar number" is actually a range of numbers with parameters that he and others are still debating.

Dunbar's theory is actively contested. Still, the numbers have had various practical applications and despite their simplicity have often been deemed useful.

The primary number, 150, is said to roughly describe the outermost limit of stable, casual social relationships a person can maintain. For good friends Dunbar's number is about 50, for close friends, 15, and for family and intimates, 5.

Whether or not those exact numbers prove robust over time—the 150 number makes me feel distinctly unpopular—Dunbar's idea that our minds engage best with each other in small groups, rather than crowds, has an observable strength. We focus most intently on those who are nearby: those we know by their bodies, their gestures, their voices, and their responses to those same aspects of ourselves.

The distant others in our lives have an abstract quality that offers us less basis for attachment—they shade into obscurity, an intangible, undifferentiated cloud. Though our intimates and friends may irritate and frustrate us, and though we feel the strain and friction of our desires' collision with their own, those close to us are the beloved.

Partly we choose to live in the foreground because it's tactile and immediate and more gratifying than the far horizon.

But socially, and possibly neurologically, we're also built that way. It may be that our minds can't keep pace with our proliferation, that we're failing to adapt, in our cognitive capacity for empathy, to our swift upsizing—the throngs of billions to which we now belong.

5

AS A PLOT POINT, a dramatizer, collateral damage, or pure spectacle, the event of death populates our tales abundantly. In action movies, for instance, minor characters die in ecstatic frenzies of destruction—human bowling pins struck by multiple, fast-moving balls. Mostly in the form of bullets or explosions.

When the extras die like this, none of us are surprised. Or even affected. It was always their role to die.

Unnoticed and unlamented, too: popular movies rarely include mourning. Grief can start a story, propelling the action forward as a main character learns to leave grief behind. But it functions mostly as a catalyst—mourning, in story structures like these, is an error of affect that needs to be corrected. And will be, before the movie ends.

Grief cannot be allowed to stop us. In our forward movement.

For to finish a story in grief, as surely as finishing it in death, defies the rule of happy endings.

As well as the rules of salesmanship, since grief is hard to sell.

Our denial of death is an integral part of the insistence on happy endings: few of us care to be reminded of the fact that every story—or every true story of personhood, anyway—has to end that way.

All plots tend to move deathward, wrote the novelist Don DeLillo in *White Noise.*

ARGUABLY THE MOST POPULAR narrative of them all is that of
Jesus, which, at first glance, lacks the kind of happy ending we've come
to demand. For in the story a good man dies at the age of thirty-three,
nailed to a torture device.

Only, now wait! Wait a few days, after this terrible death, and lo, he
is risen. Happy after all.

His tragedy is transmuted into martyrdom as an article of faith—in
Jesus's sacrifice, intention was everything. Submitting calmly to his fate
by neither fighting nor fleeing, he made his choice willingly, for the sake
of others. His suffering was not an accident but a purposeful gesture—
his pain was an offering, his crucifixion an act of heroism in the guise
of victimhood.

Jesus was a god, healing the sick, feeding the many from little, and
raising a widow's son from the dead. Like the prophet Elisha in the Torah.
He walked on water but perished like a man, flanked by the humblest
of sinners. Suffered and rose and rose again, brimming with the divinity
latent in all people and shining down through the centuries as a gift to
the faithful.

The narrative of one who suffers for many is dear to us. And told
more widely than any other single story.

WALKING ON WATER is impossible for mammals. But more than
a thousand kinds of other animals perform this feat daily. Some glide,
not breaking the water's surface tension—from water striders to pygmy
geckos—and some step.

Various aquatic insects release a surfactant, a chemical compound
that reduces surface tension between the water and their bodies, to pro-
pel themselves forward. Other species, including lizards named for Jesus
himself, are referred to as "slappers" because they're too heavy not to
break the surface tension and have to stay in motion constantly. Momentum carries them.

Several kinds of animals appear to walk on water when really they're relying on their wings or tails to hold them aloft. Port River dolphins are adept at "tail walking," moving vertically across the water with only their tails submerged.

The insects known as water striders have terrifically thin, long legs, built to distribute their slight weight across the water's surface. Their bodies are lined with "hydrofuge" hairs that stop them from getting wet and sinking.

Much of what we know about the very small creatures among us we've learned quite recently. Around 30 years BC, the Roman scholar Marcus Terentius Varro proposed the existence of microorganisms, warning his contemporaries to avoid walking around near swamps.

For in such places, he wrote, "are bred certain minute creatures which cannot be seen by the eyes, but which float in the air and enter the body through the mouth and nose and cause serious diseases."

But no one ran with his odd little theory until the 1600s, when the first powerful microscopes were built. Robert Hooke, a polymath of deep talents (he also discovered the law of elasticity, which is named for him), used his own microscope to observe the fruiting bodies of molds in 1665. He published the first illustration of one, a blue mold growing on leather, in his *Micrographia*.

Antonie van Leeuwenhoek, who owned a textile business in the Netherlands, made microscopes that allowed him to describe bacteria in 1676. He also looked at single-celled plants and animals, which he called "animalcules." And observed the spermatozoa of amphibians, birds, fish, mammals, and mollusks, concluding that fertilization occurred when sperm entered an egg.

WE PLAYED A word game in early grade school. Forty years later, at least one of my kids would play it, too.

This is the land of opposites, was what you said to start gameplay. The cue signaled that anything said by those playing the game actually meant its opposite. Then you'd try to catch out the other kids when they forgot the situation, said something wrong, and looked foolish.

If we were in the land of opposites and *I* forgot, and another kid mentioned a friendless boy in our class and accused me of liking him, I might say, No, I definitely don't have a crush on that boy.

Opposite! It's the opposite! She has a crush on him! the leader would taunt. She said it! She said so!

I meant, I *do* have a crush on him.

But suddenly, arbitrarily and capriciously, the leader would declare that we weren't in the land of opposites anymore.

You heard it! She has a crush on him!

Then the others might join together in the dreaded singsong jeer: *Liddy and So-and-so, sitting in a tree, K-I-S-S-I-N-G! First comes love, then comes marriage, then comes Liddy pushing the BABY carriage!*

The game was a power grab: the rules of language got changed on you by whoever seized the reins.

It was guaranteed, sooner or later, to piss someone off.

THE STORY OF one man's sacrifice for all is a tale from the land of opposites—a stark symbolic reversal of social reality. Since in almost all the orders established by our kind, the many have suffered for the few.

And in practical terms, we continue to believe in human sacrifice. As well as the sacrifice of other animals.

Not voluntary, as Jesus's was, but forced.

The forms of those sacrifices are anodyne these days, distributed over a vague and abstract backdrop. Embedded in neutral phrases like *market forces* and *structural inequity*—formalized through the decisions of institutions, described in the jargon of economic trade-offs.

Still the pain of others remains the offering, the suffering it alleviates our own.

"GREATER LOVE HATH no man than this," wrote John in his Gospel, "that he lay down his life for his friend."

There's a lonely beauty in the idea—the pathos of a supreme generosity. But honestly, to lay down our life for anyone isn't among our goals.

The story of Jesus can be seen as one where the son of God, in his selfless sacrifice, stands in for the many rather than the one—for all of us in our personal suffering. But it remains, clearly, an epic with a lone hero: the greatest story ever told centers around an individual—not a woman, of course, though Jesus has a devoted mother and a female disciple to witness his rising from the tomb—and not a group of people. But one man.

This is the case with most of the legends and myths we elevate.

In faith, including the one Jesus inspired, the self is called upon to subsume itself into the whole. But without a community of faith, that drive toward the greater good recedes. And stories bend themselves toward the glory of a single person. Without the practice of submission to a divine other—who represents, ideally, a commitment to social duty and a common moral scheme—the collective fades into a distant feature of the landscape.

Without a call to prayer, maybe that glorification of the individual hero becomes a faith of its own.

FOR SOME FIVE HUNDRED YEARS the booths of confessionals, in Roman Catholic churches, have welcomed penitents in search of absolution.

In my late teens, when I got to visit cathedrals in France and Italy and Spain, I was so taken by them I wished to be a member of the congregation instead of a lowly tourist: their beauty was enrapturing. The design of those ancient buildings is brilliant—a binary in spiritual tension. Above and below, sacred and profane, collective and private. Tall windows filter sunbeams cast from the sky, saturated in the colors of stained glass and streaming their holy light. Motes of dust drift in the rays, bathing the bowed heads of the worshippers in the pews. Sheltered from the elements but lifted up by the illumination of the heavens.

Below there are the dark closets, where the faithful go to have their mistakes laid bare. To expose their dealings with the baser forces, they're ushered into dim, private boxes for an audience with God's intermediaries. From up high comes a rectifying light, encompassing the gathered assembly; down low rests the sectioned-off and secret darkness, the cubbies of self-revelation and of sin.

In these cubbies, through nothing but speech, a person's errors can be revealed. And touched by the finger of forgiveness.

Which is available only through spoken words. Requests for help called prayers, the penance of Hail Marys and Our Fathers.

Language is the key to our redemption.

I say "our" with a kind of wistfulness, extending myself into the crowd. I longed to enter the seclusion of those old, wooden-smelling booths and whisper my dark secrets—the sin of envy, possibly.

But I could not: their sanctuary was denied to the likes of me. Due to, not a Catholic.

EVEN AS AN ADULT I would suffer, in certain moments, from an envy of religiosity. Once, in a car with my friend Kate and my then-husband Kierán—who'd been raised Jewish and Catholic, respectively—I listened to them tell fond, eccentric stories of their religious upbringings in the front seat and, in the back seat, began to feel tears filling my eyes.

By and by Kate turned around and saw me.

"Lydia's crying!" she exclaimed.

They asked me why, and I muttered something about feeling left out. They only laughed; it was funny to them. Or at least absurd.

I felt injured—it wasn't that I wanted to believe, but that I wanted to belong.

PERSONAL CONFESSION, FOLLOWING Freud and his successors, moved beyond the Catholic Church that had once cornered the market.

And then, in social media and the generations raised with it, into the public domain.

More and more of us reveled in confession, during the century after Freud. We relish the exposure and disrobing of the hidden heart.

Many wear the offenses committed against them, as well as their successes, like badges that flash when they catch the light. A bling of injury and triumph that forges and broadcasts their identity.

Some of us are drawn to an identity of woundedness, others to one of entitlement. Some wish to prove their suffering is real, while others wish to deny the evidence of others' suffering. And to show, through that denial, that they are the greater sufferers.

The struggle is over who suffers most. And who should be rewarded for it.

ALONG WITH THE therapists' chairs and confessionals there are bars, where no religious affiliation is required and only a modest supply of cash. Many are equipped with their own dark booths where we can sit and speak.

Women, in general, are the designated listeners—when emotions and relationships are the subject, even my male friends mostly prefer to unburden themselves to women.

Maybe this is because, outside the formal structures of confession, women are the standard-bearers of support and nurturing; maybe we're also perceived as less threatening and less competitive; or maybe it's purely practical and has to do with the fact that many women are patient with long-winded introspection. And, speaking for myself at least, entertained by reports of interpersonal drama.

In the bars, along with alcohol, confidence is on offer. And much confiding occurs. We raise our glasses and offer an accounting of the week's or month's misdeeds. Our setbacks and gaffes, at work and at play. The beer and wine and liquor fill us with warmth and make our boundaries fluid: when the spirits enter us we turn magnanimous—more willing to expose our injuries, more sympathetic to the injuries of others.

In the bars we're both together and separate—among the congregation and in the confessionals at once.

And our friends make excellent confessors. Because you don't have to be perfect to serve as an arbiter of right and wrong.

We know that from the priests.

Of course, certain church features are absent there. Including the figure of an emaciated man with a lovely face, naked except for a loincloth, dripping his crimson blood on two crossed timbers.

In the bars we seldom miss him.

6
—

WE LIKE TO CONFESS, but we like to keep secrets, too.

I work for a conservation group staffed by scientists, lawyers, activists, and communications specialists like me, along with the fundraisers and admin and IT employees whose efforts enable the rest. At my work—and across the science and environmental communities more broadly—a deep anxiety took hold, in the final decades of the twentieth century. A form of stultifying panic too fundamental to be calmly expressed.

As the fossil fuel complex spent lavishly to discredit the notion of climate change, the knowledge of it vibrated with an electric urgency among those of us who were paying rapt attention. Yet in public conversation, even on those occasions when pieces of information surfaced, they weren't received with a sense of emergency. Often they were treated as a niche preoccupation rather than an existential threat.

In some of the circles I moved in, among biologists and atmospheric scientists and environmentalists, the climate and extinction crises were a source of primal fear—factual givens that overwhelmed us in their demand for a political response.

But in other circles I knew a bit, like media and publishing and Hollywood, they retained the quality of a boutique interest. As though the fearful belonged to an obscure affinity group or a collection of hobbyists.

Pressing concern with the "issues" of global warming or mass extinction betrayed an earnestness that was far less fashionable than detachment.

We faced a double menace, in the subcultures that were ringing the alarm bells: the danger itself, which filled us with dread, and laid atop it the weight of its cloak of invisibility—a gaslighting that was binding us all to a grim future.

Held in abeyance by a willful ignorance, the climate catastrophe and cascade of extinctions were a public secret whose knowing was disavowed. Public secrecy is at the core of power, as the anthropologist Michael Taussig wrote in *Defacement*. But it's also at the core of powerlessness, since wherever there is power there is its negative. Which stretches over all of us, outside the hot centers where true power lies.

Over decades, along with corporations and governments, the cultural mythmakers refused to give the climate and extinction crises a place in their storytelling. They drummed their fingers on their knees, directing our attention to brighter and more spectacular diversions.

Among the diversions were blockbuster movies and popular TV shows of various forms of apocalypse. The asteroid, meteorite, or comet apocalypse. The sun-goes-supernova apocalypse. The human-sterility apocalypse. The sudden-ice-age apocalypse. The volcano, tsunami, or earthquake apocalypse. The giant-scary-animal apocalypse. The robot-cyborg apocalypse. The alien-invasion apocalypse. The radioactive-monster apocalypse. The cannibal-zombie apocalypse. The AI apocalypse.

Any apocalypse but our own.

Maybe those hyped-up fictions functioned as a psychological vaccine against the actual disease. The more outrageous and cathartic the story, the greater its power to reassure us that an apocalypse is fantasy.

Persistently, in parts of our culture and parts of the psyche, the idea of *apocalypse* shivers with an ominous weight—a sword that hangs on a delicate thread above us, always and never dropping.

Unreal, surreal, and hyperreal.

We deny and embrace at the same time. Scoff and fear.

Disbelieve and believe.

THE ONES WHO came before us marked the passing of days and seasons by the sun and moon. The presence or absence, and the behavior, of animals and plants around them. Back then time was often seen as a circle or a spiral: births and deaths that recurred, disappearances and reappearances, over and over in cycles.

As moderns who live indoors, cut off from the soil and sky—and emerge mostly to move along surfaces that are similarly separated from the ground, their uniform covering a mixture of processed rocks and oil—we tend to place ourselves beyond those cycles. Alongside them, at best. We tolerate their occurrence and make minor adjustments, but often we barely feel them. Who can blame us? Electricity replicates daylight when the dark of night is inconvenient; homes are heated or cooled to keep them feeling much the same in summer as they do in winter. In our custom-made spaces the changing of seasons and the planet's rotation are sidelined.

This exclusion of natural processes is fragile and temporary, as we recognize with an affronted shock when suddenly overcome by the smoke of wildfires or the flooding of storms.

Even a simple, brief power loss. Or a broken air conditioner or furnace.

Out in my own home, in the desert outside Tucson, the sporadic disappearance of access to the internet—in our case, conveyed to a receiver on our roof by radio signals—is a bleak event. When it happens the household exists in a state of limbo. And resentment. Our sudden, rude disconnection blocks us from everything we have to do. And much of what we want to. My son can't play Minecraft, my daughter can't finish her homework or watch old episodes of *Parks and Recreation*, and I can't conduct research on the sex habits of spiny echidnas.

Most great cities are far more vulnerable to the uncontainment of nature than we like to believe. New York, as the journalist Alan Weisman pointed out in a 2007 book called *The World Without Us*, is built atop rushing subterranean rivers and would be swamped in days if its pumps were abandoned.

But for now, in the urban world, we live in regulated spaces—strictly measured out and separated, keeping individuals and classes where the laws and routines of property and commerce want them to be.

Time is a series of compartments too, more and more precisely standardized and globalized over the course of modern history. The monthly, weekly, daily, and hourly increments of forward movement are a structure of temporal confinement, regimenting our daily behavior with such conceptual hardness that even our mental picture of time takes the shape of a grid. Our visual representation of this, the squares or rectangles arranged on our calendars in straight lines, has displaced more fluid and circular notions of seasonality.

Both space and time have been transformed into right-angled shapes, so that our thoughts, as well as our bodies, occur inside rows of boxes.

I live in "July" or on "Sunday"—inside the language and squared-off units of time—with more immediacy than in the sensed experience of high summer or the rising and setting of the spheres. Even the names of days have stories and characters, pegged to routines of work and leisure and sleep.

Tell me why I don't like Mondays. Hump Days are always tough. Thank *God* it's Friday.

The grid gives us a feeling of control over our doings, a coping tool that allows us to self-regulate—to manage, say, the duties of employment and child-rearing and housekeeping. But meanwhile it superimposes itself on the night-and-day, growth-and-death cycles of the actual living world, neatly replacing the essential movements of planetary existence with an industrial, human-built narrative of time. Suppressing, for instance, the circadian rhythms that regulate the twenty-four-hour cycles of our biological clocks in favor of an artificial construct of manufactured light and darkness.

Only a few of us can recognize or define the equinoxes or solstices. Only a few know how the sun tracks across the sky at different times of year, how the angle of its light changes.

We see the moon in the sky. We notice when winter and spring arrive.

But do we know why the face of the moon is always turned toward us? Can we tell our children how there come to be seasons at all?

ROUND, BRISTLY, AND cuddly-looking like hedgehogs, spiny echidnas share a bony hind-leg spur with male platypuses—the only other mammals that lay eggs. While platypus spurs secrete a toxin so strong that it can kill a dog, the echidnas' release a harmless, waxy substance.

What male echidnas lack in poison, though, they make up for in mating eccentricities. They form lines of up to ten males behind a female, with each male's long, skinny snout nudging up against the rump ahead of it, and wait for the female to be ready.

This waddling procession, which can last for six weeks, has been called a "mating train" and a "love train." During the wait some males drop out and others take their place. When the female's finally in the mood, they dig a donut-shaped trench around her and tussle for the honor of intercourse by pushing each other out of the hollow they've created. *We shall fight in the trenches.*

When a victor prevails, it's time for the deployment of his four-headed penis. He only uses two heads at a time, since the female has just two cavities available. One echidna, retired from zoo service because of his propensity for displaying his erections during educational viewing sessions, was studied and recorded by Steve Johnston of the University of Queensland. This exhibitionist can be seen on video by those not worried about the browser repercussions of searching "four-headed penis."

The resulting egg is hatched inside the female's pouch—echidnas have pouches like marsupials—and when the baby echidna, or "puggle," begins to grow spines, it emerges from the pouch and is nursed to maturity.

Echidnas have a lower body temperature than any other mammal and a slow metabolism. They can live for upwards of forty-five years and harbor the world's largest known flea, which is named after them: *Bradiopsylla echidnae.*

ALL THE EGG-LAYING MAMMALS—four echidna species and the duck-billed platypus—live in Australia.

The first European naturalist to examine a platypus specimen

assumed it was a hoax, the eighteenth-century equivalent of the "Fee-
jee Mermaid" later displayed by P. T. Barnum, which was a gruesome,
dried-up taxidermy hybrid of ape and fish parts, or the jackalope first
popularized in the United States in the 1930s—a jackrabbit with antlers
affixed to its head.

This naturalist, George Shaw, wrote in 1799 that the creature had
the body of a quadruped but the bill and webbed feet of a duck. (It
also seemed to have the tail of a beaver.) Some joker could easily have
stuck the pieces together and shipped the thing from Australia in a fit of
profit-making mischief.

The debate over platypuses would go on for almost a century, with
thousands of corpses sent back to Europe to satisfy the inquisitive.

FROM MY HOUSE I can walk to rock-art pictures of spirals, among
other petroglyphs that dot this desert valley at thousands of different
sites. They're believed to have been made by the Hohokam between five
hundred and fifteen hundred years ago.

Spirals show up repeatedly in the ancient Native American rock art of
the Southwest and may have played different roles for different cultures,
from denoting water sources to marking human migrations.

Most of the symbols' meanings are not known to those outside the
cultures of the living tribes. But archaeologists believe some were designed
and positioned to capture sunlight only at the solstices and equinoxes.

BACK WHEN CIRCULAR TIME was the story we told, human time
was also plant and animal time. It followed the flowering and fruiting
of trees and bushes and fungi, their dormancy in winter. It followed the
migrations of beasts or their hibernation and reemergence in spring.

In those days we had gods and demigods who, with the rest of the natural world, were born and died and reborn. In an endlessly repeating cycle.

Among them was Osiris in Egyptian myth and Dionysus and Adonis in Greek, along with Ishtar and Persephone. Tammuz in Mesopotamian legend, Baldr and Hodr in Norse.

Jesus was of this lineage—a demigod, half man and half divine, who perished and rose again. As so many of the old gods had.

But the Bible supplied an ending for all the sons and daughters of God: the Revelation to John. A single powerful, rageful book, among all the different and often gentler books of the New Testament, that foretold the end of human history.

And reads like a madman's fever dream of battle and vengeance.

John's Book of Revelation has predicted since about 96 AD that the reign of humankind will culminate in a violent finale: an apocalypse, the Greek word for "revelation." On that bloody day of reckoning, when the messiah returns, those Christians with an end-times bent will at last reap the rewards of their correct opinions.

Some welcome the signs; Southern Baptists support Zionist military programs as a necessary step toward the Second Coming of Christ. For the Rapture will follow an epic holy war in the Middle East.

So the vision of salvation is predicated on the destruction of the known world. And all who live in it.

Portents of that destruction, like rising seas and red tides, animal die-offs and fires and famines besetting unbelievers, are not to be feared but ushered in gratefully—elements of a plotline that confirms the imminence of the true kingdom.

Out of the ashes the chosen will rise like phoenixes. And when tomorrow comes they will be called to sit, in the endless time after the end of time, at the right hand of God.

EVEN TO THOSE OF US within Judeo-Christian culture who don't anticipate the Rapture, time looks more like a line than a circle. It marches forward. And will finally leave us behind.

Because a circle goes on and on, if you follow its curve. But a straight line can have an end point. So the story we tell, in our straight-line version of history, has a beginning, a middle, and an end. Linear time is a function, some have argued, of the apocalyptic model of story.

Maybe, with the advent of linear time, we talked ourselves out of the eternal.

And had to propose an afterlife to talk our way back in.

Back into forever—the only happy ending that lasts.

7

THE SWEDISH TAXONOMIST Carl Linnaeus was the one who named us *Homo sapiens*, "wise man." He was so powerful and respected in his lifetime, in the 1700s, that he was able to send students all over the globe to collect botanical specimens. He called the students his "apostles"— half jokingly, it seems.

Their expeditions were hazardous: of the seventeen apostles who set out, seven never returned, falling to illnesses against which they had no immunity. And sometimes to alcohol or opium addiction.

Linnaeus was the first to group human beings, *Homo*, with apes, *Simia*. He saw people as members of the animal kingdom, a view that was highly controversial. As Darwin's work would soon be, catalyzing an evolution vs. creation debate that continues—from the perspective of that subset of Christians who cleave to a particular understanding of the literal truth of the Bible—in the United States today.

"Young earth" creationism pegs the age of the earth at around six thousand years, following the biblical arithmetic of a seventeenth-century Irish churchman named James Ussher. Because Ussher's six-thousand-year math runs up against the evidence of evolution (and the findings of archaeology, paleontology, astrophysics, and scientific inquiry in general), Darwin remains a popular villain to young-earth creationists.

Across the United States, car-bumper ornaments—usually stickers

made of silver-painted plastic—do battle over the idea of evolution. I see
them almost daily as I drive.

A stylized fish representing Christ is the opening salvo, professing the
faith of a car's driver. It reminds me of the BABY ON BOARD signs suc-
tioned to rear windows, which ask drivers behind a vehicle to curb their
presumably aggressive impulses.

The lives of other occupants are, apparently, less valuable.

CHRISTIAN ON BOARD, says the fish.

In retaliation, on secular-owned cars, the fish is given legs,
symbolizing evolution.

Then the fish with legs is emblazoned, on still other cars, with the
word *Jesus*. Perhaps this signals the driver *is* Christian, but pro-evolution.

Next the word *Darwin* or *Science* is substituted for *Jesus*.

Sometimes creationism gets the last word: two fish are combined, one
eating the other. The small fish, with one tiny leg visible as it enters the
mouth of the big one, says *Darwin* on it. The big, legless Jesus fish that's
eating it says *Truth*.

Young-earth creationism is a rejection of metaphor in Scripture, seeing figurative readings of the Bible as a threat to its holiness and hege-
mony. Such readings seem to undermine the infallibility of the Word,
representing a treacherous slide down the road to a loss of faith.

Rather than, say, attesting to the human imperfection, or simple
fondness for poetry, of God's mortal messengers.

TO MANY OF HIS ERA, Linnaeus's placing of humankind on a continuum with apes was an insult to God and people alike.

In his book *Dieta Naturalis*, he wrote: "One should not vent one's
wrath on animals, Theology decree that man has a soul and that animals are mere 'automata mechanica,' but I believe they would be better
advised that animals have a soul and that the difference is of nobility."

On the matter of the animal soul, even the father of hierarchical taxonomy himself was willing to extend the benefit of the doubt.

DEFINED AS THE psyche or spirit, soul, at its root, is the breath of life. The movement of air entering a body and leaving it again, invisible by itself but with the power to animate. But we invest *soul* with both broader and narrower meanings—broader than breath and narrower than life. Notions of soul carry intimations of immortality, of a self that persists after breathing has ceased.

The Bible doesn't say that animals are without a soul or have a different soul from people. "What happens to the children of man and what happens to the beasts is the same," reads Ecclesiastes 3:19. "As one dies, so dies the other. They all have the same breath, and man has no advantage over the beasts, for all is vanity."

In practice, though, most churches maintain a distinction: If an animal soul does exist, it dies with the animal's body. While the human soul can live on outside its material host.

Otherwise, come to think of it, what use would faith be?

THE IDEA OF animal suicide has interested us since antiquity. In his *History of Animals*, Aristotle wrote of a stallion who realized he'd mated with his mother, much like Oedipus in the play by Sophocles. Presumably understanding that he'd violated a horse-culture taboo, he hurled himself into an abyss.

In modern media we often tell stories of dogs whose devotion to their masters is so profound that they lie down on their graves to follow them into death, as in the 2011 Australian movie *Red Dog*.

Perhaps, we think, other animals can waste away from sheer love. All the more heartrending when it's unrequited—as with Nigel, a gannet who was lured to New Zealand's Mana Island with gannet decoys by biologists hoping to establish a colony of the birds there.

For years Nigel lived alone on the island, with no other real gannets and only the decoys for friends. He chose one of them as a mate, doing his best to groom her cold, concrete feathers.

After a while three other real gannets arrived on the island. But Nigel ignored them and died next to his unliving mate, in the fine nest he'd built for her.

Animal suicides, we've been given to understand, can also be caused by group insanity—lemmings rushing in hordes off cliffs into the sea are cited as a prime example.

In fact suicidal lemmings are a fabrication: in the 1958 Walt Disney "documentary" *White Wilderness*, which popularized the myth, lemmings—small rodents that migrate when population pressure drives them to seek new territories—were apparently purchased, spun around on a snow-covered turntable, then chased off a precipice by the filmmakers.

Whether this cinematic manipulation was intended to showcase the irrationality of beasts or simply seen as good drama is unclear.

We tell ourselves stories about other animals who wish to end their own lives, as some people do, while simultaneously telling ourselves another tale that lets us off the hook—that animals have little access to feeling and no understanding of personal death, lacking the self-awareness and abstract thinking that might allow them to conceive of it. Our emotional instincts about the others lead us toward empathy and identification, but both of these we also rationalize away: the difference of animals confuses us.

Historically we've often executed animals for infractions of a nature we deem to be criminal or spiritually wrong. In the animal trials of Europe, at least from the Middle Ages on, people held the beasts responsible for violations of human ethical codes, clearly conferring moral agency on them. In France, for example, it was once common for domestic animals—and some wild ones—to be tried by law and put to death or excommunicated by the church for their acts.

These animal trials, which occurred from the twelfth century onward, took place in both secular and ecclesiastical courts. Those tried and punished ranged from all manner of mammals to reptiles and insects. Large animals were often executed for hurting or killing people—pigs, most frequently, when they trampled children or, in 1864 in Croatia, bit off a baby's ears—while small ones like insects and parasites were excommunicated because they were bothersome.

For people, excommunication means exclusion from participation in church—not a harsh punishment for your average insect or worm. In the case of animal pests, it was likely intended to serve as permission for people to kill them, since once excommunicated they no longer had to be treated gently, the way God's creations otherwise should.

As E. P. Evans, still the preeminent documenter of animal trials, wrote in his 1906 book *The Criminal Prosecution and Capital Punishment of Animals*, some were even "put to the rack" and tortured—more or less as a procedural formality, since no confession was anticipated.

In the early twentieth century there was the famous case of Topsy the circus elephant, who was difficult to handle and killed a man (after he burned her with a cigar). Notably, her reputation as a man-killer brought in large crowds and revenues for the circus.

Still, she was high maintenance, and her hard-drinking keeper went AWOL after a while. So Topsy was put to death publicly at Coney Island in 1903—by multiple means, including cyanide poisoning, electrocution, and strangling with weighted ropes for good measure. The punitive nature of this killing implied both guilt and retribution, and her execution was well attended.

The fact that these trials lasted so far into modernity may stand as a testimony to the reluctance of Western society to fully relinquish its hold on the nearness of beasts—to a centuries-long conflict within ourselves over the other animals' ongoing reduction into objects.

CHIMPS AND BONOBOS are our closest living relatives, sharing almost 99 percent of our DNA, while gorillas share about 98 and orangutans 97. The ancestors of all primates showed up after the non-avian dinosaurs were wiped out some 66 million years ago. They were small at first, like rats or squirrels, but over time they grew.

Between 8 million and 4 million years back, gorilla and chimp forebears diverged from the lineage that led to *Homo sapiens*. Recently, in evolutionary time, people started making art; they were painting on cave walls forty-five thousand years ago.

But so far there's no agreement on when we turned into us.

Many human characteristics have been named as hallmarks of our specialness. These include the creation of abstract symbols and development of written languages, the ability to reason, the capacity for group cooperation, and the awareness of a distant past and future. Also our opposable thumbs combined with bipedal uprightness, our handiness with fire and habit of cooking food before we eat it, our production of music and art, our concepts of God, and our laughter.

The litany of human distinctions is so long it starts to look like a résumé. With, at the bottom of the page—that brief, indulgently personal section that often seems laughably irrelevant to potential employers— titled "Other Skills."

- First species to weaponize a tiny particle known as the atom.
- First species to weaponize the sun.
- And the air.
- And the fossils.
- And the ocean, from which all life emerged.

THOSE WHO DRAW parallels between human and beastly behavior are often accused of "anthropomorphism," the bad habit of imbuing other animals with human motivations. Biologists are shamed when they do this—their objectivity is questioned. A condescending kiss of death, even in postmodern times where "objective" science has been proven a flawed paradigm.

And it's true that we can't say, when another kind of animal "exhibits" a given behavior (say, mating face to face, as humans and bonobos do), that it does so for the same reasons a human might "exhibit" that behavior.

But there's a fallacy in the accusation. While it may be irrational to draw conclusions about an animal's motivations from its acts, it's equally irrational to presume that people have exclusive access to impulses like love or jealousy—that these are primarily human impulses.

It's far more likely that emotions such as affection and desire are distributed liberally among complex organisms, like other functions of neural and hormonal circuitry and social conditioning. That what Linnaeus described as a "difference of nobility" between human and animal souls is less a difference of hierarchy or merit than a difference of kind. And that imputing deep emotions to other creatures is not a forced comparison to the parochial standard of *us*, but part of a larger pattern-finding—a wider search into an abyss of information we've barely begun to plumb.

The way many children respond to animals—not only with curiosity and delight, but also with a sense of companionship and instinctive solidarity that tends to disregard or minimize the boundaries between species—has an experiential authenticity that should inform the perspectives of biological inquiry instead of being dismissed.

Practiced with thoughtfulness and circumspection, the act some call "anthropomorphic" may simply be a gesture of inclusiveness that sees common experience as a valid framework for learning—a pathway as rich with potential as those we've relied on so long, in the sciences, that work through separation and exclusion.

WHEN I WAS a kid and had a pet guinea pig who died, I stood for hours near her cage, where the round, furry body lay, staring into a corner of the room. Weeping, I asked my parents if anyone had ever committed suicide because their guinea pig died.

They considered the question politely, as they passed me at my appointed station of mourning. Then said, Probably not.

However, they conceded, they didn't have all the facts at their disposal. It was possible that some child suicides caused by deceased guinea pigs had not been reported as such. Flown under the radar, they said.

Self-murder wasn't a realistic option for me at the time—I liked my life and had few violent impulses beyond wanting to pinch the soft skin of my little brother with sharp, raggedly bitten fingernails. This was natural, since he had stolen the attention that was rightfully mine. So I was grandstanding, but my abjection was genuine.

Hiccup-sobbing, I saw that I'd betrayed Trudy. Avoided cleaning the droppings that piled up on her pee-soaked newspaper and bed of cedar shavings. Consigned her to a squalid life in a cage that was not unlike a toilet. Often fed her only dry pellets from the plastic food bag, too lazy to walk to the fridge and pick off a leaf of fresh lettuce. Which she demonstrably preferred.

I'd even said to myself, on more than one occasion, She's just a guinea pig. She doesn't mind.

But I hadn't conceived of that rationalization independently, I'd realize later: I was mimicking what I'd heard. From older people, when they talked about the other animals. He's just a ———. She's just a ———. Oh, don't worry, they are only ———.

Shame constricted my throat.

If I'd known, right then, about the flagellants—who whipped their bare backs with sharp implements in mass marches through cities beginning in thirteenth-century Italy—I would have gone looking for a procession.

As it was, I gave up my mourning after some hours had elapsed and abandoned my position staring at the wall. It had gotten boring, and I was quite hungry.

But I never forgot the feeling of loss. Or the guilt over my neglect: how I had let them reassure me.

She's only a guinea pig.

MY LITTLE BROTHER and sister and I buried numerous family pets behind our house, along with a couple of wild birds we found, in shoebox coffins or T-shirt shrouds.

Sometimes we said a few words; sometimes we were silent.

But there was always a gravity to the passing and honoring of these smaller beings.

MANY AMONG US, now, have an inkling of what lies ahead if we stay on the path we've made, with its deep ruts keeping the wheels in place. But as far as we can tell, the beasts have not received the news.

There's evidence, here and there, that some of them are adapting to changing conditions like temperature and rainfall. Mylene Mariette, a behavioral ecologist in Australia, has found that some finches communicate with the embryos inside their eggs, which can hear, and learn from, outside sounds.

Her research has shown that finch parents utter certain sounds only when maximum daily temperatures exceed 79 degrees Fahrenheit. Chicks exposed to those calls go on to hatch with lower birth weights than control embryos not exposed to the calls, and are themselves more vocal. That lower birth weight is an advantage in hot weather, making it easier for the birds to cool down. Also, when those lower-weight chicks were kept at higher temperatures than the control chicks after hatching, they produced more fledglings.

Mariette suggests this finch behavior may be helping the birds adapt to warming.

But numerous species may not prove able to adapt at a pace that matches the rapid rate of change. Some biologists have suggested that those in the tropics, for instance, will prove less adaptable to change than those that live farther from the equator—they've evolved without substantial variations in temperature and haven't needed to develop behavioral or genetic methods for dealing with such variation.

Unfortunately, the tropics are where most species live.

Also, since evolution occurs over multiple generations, it's possible that species with short lifespans and fast reproduction, which are typically small-bodied, will have advantages over the larger ones that take many years to reproduce. Fruit flies multiply and die quickly, having a lifespan around two weeks, so adaptation may go fairly well for them.

Large animals—many of whom are already rare or endangered—may not be able to rely on adaptive mechanisms in time to survive.

And many beasts are constrained by warmth or coolness in their biology. Animals including sea turtles, alligators, and crocodiles are subject to the process of "temperature-dependent sex determination."

When sea turtle eggs incubate below about 82 degrees Fahrenheit, they develop into males. Above about 88 degrees, females. Between those two temperatures, a mix. This means the warming climate could produce all-female young among populations of any or all of these animals. In which case whole species could wink out abruptly.

On the Great Barrier Reef, in the Pacific Ocean's largest green sea turtle rookery, the population, in 2020, was 80 percent female.

But its young turtles were 99 percent female.

So sea turtles—who already lived when *T. rex* roamed the land and swam with ichthyosaurs and plesiosaurs—would seem to be in acute peril. Seven species of these ocean-crossing migrants still abide, having diverged from extinct forms about 110 million years ago. They're among the most ancient, still-living large creatures we know. Six of their seven species are already endangered, and their epic migrations across the globe make them hard to protect.

They take decades to reach sexual maturity, and though they lay about a hundred eggs at a time, only one of those hatchlings typically survives to reproduce.

The largest among them are leatherbacks, which grow up to six and a half feet long.

One female leatherback, tracked by satellite in 2007, made a journey from Indonesia to Oregon—more than 12,700 miles.

TYRANNOSAURUS REX, THE king of dinosaurs, is famous for its large, ferocious teeth and tiny, dangling arms. Children now know so many dinosaurs and pterosaurs and ichthyosaurs it's almost impossible to keep up with them. During his early dinosaur phase, Silas could rhyme off the names of fossilized specimens I had never heard of and would indignantly correct me about the differences between certain ancient marine reptiles and flying lizards and "true" dinosaurs.

My knowledge was sadly outmoded: when I was little, in the seventies, dino-celebrity had been simpler. We all knew of *T. rex* and we all knew of the *Brontosaurus*, or "thunder lizard," which was temporarily erased from paleontology and later tentatively resurrected. The two of them were bookends: a mean, scary meat-eater and a giant, blunt-toothed herbivore with a long neck.

In our playroom, my brother and sister and I made their plastic replicas have fights, which consisted of us banging them together while issuing threats.

I'll kill you, stupid T. rex. I'll step on you and squash you. No I'll kill *you*, you Brontosaurus, and then I'll eat your head.

Historically their existence on the planet was separated by some 100 million years.

ICHTHYOSAURS BODIES' RESEMBLED dolphins, and they're believed to have hunted in groups, as dolphins do, though they're not closely related. As with today's cetaceans—in a case of "convergent evolution"—they were land animals for a while.

Then they returned to the sea.

THERE ARE SO MANY codes we haven't broken yet that we can't determine with any degree of certainty what the beasts or the green lifeforms do or don't understand. We can observe their behavior and dissect their bodies, but our knowledge of their interior lives is in its infancy. Though we've gathered a little evidence in select cases like dolphins and great apes and the family of birds called corvids, we haven't identified in any detail who among them are self-aware.

For the vast majority of beings that aren't us, we don't know to what degree they can see themselves seeing, feel themselves feeling, or think of themselves thinking. Outside a tradition that arguably dates from the French philosopher René Descartes, we can't even pinpoint why this matters so much to us—why this metacognition is so necessary for the beasts to be given our respect.

After all, there seems to be ample social evidence that plenty of us don't regularly practice self-reflection either.

On a scale, anyway, that might improve the lives of our fellows.

We *can* say that great numbers of the beasts are able to feel and think. And be confident that in each of their varieties, in each of their physiologies and histories, lies an experience of existence that we have never had.

So what the beasts may know or sense about the catastrophic physical shifts happening around them is unknown to us. Even whether they have a concept of passing and coming time is an unanswered question. In our scientific paradigms we've always assumed they do not—that only we, in our minds, can travel through time to imagine a far-off future.

Say, the end of ourselves. Or even the end of our species.

But it's always been our habit to make convenient assumptions about subordinate classes and kinds.

Animal suffering, like animal cognition, has been the subject of much of this assuming. In past centuries, in our often violent experiments on the beasts, we liked to claim they felt no pain. To Descartes, all other animals were reflex-driven machines—automatons made of flesh—and so did not possess consciousness.

This position made it easier for him to perform the dissections of living animals for which he advocated. At his urging the practice was embraced by English scientists like Robert Hooke and Robert Boyle, who answered the call to vivisect.

Descartes defined consciousness within strict parameters, as the capacity for rational thought and for doubt rather than sensation and perception. For him, only the ability to observe one's own thought process—sometimes called metacognition—allowed for the possibility of consciousness. And the other animals do not doubt, he decided.

They might know things, the other animals—but what is knowing if you don't know you know?

In intellectual circles, Descartes's mechanistic view of animal kind would fall out of favor in the nineteenth century. Yet Cartesianism, in its privileging of deductive reasoning over sensory and emotional experience, continues to play an outsize role in our devaluation of the animal self.

WE LOVED IT ALL

Under questioning about the Iraqi dictator Saddam Hussein's purported weapons of mass destruction, Donald Rumsfeld—President George W. Bush's hawkish defense secretary—famously replied that to our intelligence services there are known knowns, known unknowns, and unknown unknowns. Things we know we know, things we know we don't know, and things we don't know we don't know.

It's in the domain of the unknown unknowns that we're at our most vulnerable. Whether as warmongers or as seekers of peace.

What Rumsfeld left out were the unknown knowns. This fourth category was cited by the philosopher Slavoj Žižek, in the Rumsfeld case, to denote denied knowledge—knowledge we have and pretend not to have.

It might also be used more simply, without implying purposeful deception, to describe what we know unconsciously but fail to acknowledge. Such as the pain of others.

The notion of the pain-free animal persisted well into the twentieth century despite a long history of people's personal experience with animals and their pain. Those of us who know them, even a little, can easily recognize that pain by their behavior. We see evidence of animal pain all over the place: when we touch a dog's hurt paw and the dog jerks her paw back quickly, we understand the dog is hurt.

What we've chosen to discount isn't the physical manifestations of pain but the emotional suffering that comes with them.

Eventually practitioners of Western science allowed that other animals *did* feel pain. And maybe even suffered.

Not as much as *we* did, of course. It would have to be a lesser pain—a duller, smaller suffering.

White enslavers and their apologists reasoned in this way to justify the torments of enslavement. And still today, in medical settings, the pain of some human patients—people of color, say, and women and the poor—is not taken as seriously as the pain of privileged classes.

Some beasts may have what we define as language; some may not. Or their systems of information transfer may be so different from our own that, so far, we haven't been able to identify or comprehend them.

Either way, we don't speak their languages. So we can't reach out of our knowledge space concerning the planet's future to tell them what's coming.

We can't say: Hurry! Prepare yourself, my dears.

We keep a terrifying secret from the others.

8
—

BIRDS IN THE corvid family—including crows and ravens—are among the most intelligent other animals that people have studied, demonstrating self-awareness in a mirror and the ability to use tools. Crows, for example, "have a theory of mind," says an ornithologist at Cornell. That is, they're able to impute emotional or mental states to others, identifying beliefs and intentions. They can recognize human faces and gaits and create compound tools out of multiple objects—a skill humans don't learn for several years after birth.

These birds' brain-to-body mass is on a par with nonhuman great apes and cetaceans—only slightly smaller than that of *Homo sapiens*. Although brain-to-body mass is a controversial metric as a predictor of intelligence.

Crows live for some twenty years in the wild, have an extended adolescence, mate for life, and live in cooperative families where older siblings sometimes help to raise younger ones. They like to play and can be mischievous, as Native American cultures have long recognized in their crow-and-raven trickster myths: they play jokes on other animals, including dogs and cats.

From which they seem to derive no material benefit. Only amusement.

IN THE SMALL HOURS of the morning, woken up by tree branches scraping on the metal roof or a sliver of moonlight leaking in through a chink in the blinds, I've tried to get a handle on loneliness. On the link between that feeling and another that often comes with it: the certainty of my own dying. The cold shadow it casts on my warm, recumbent body.

Though lying down brings relief and rest, and by allowing for sleep keeps us alive, it's also a mimicry of deadness—what we and other animals do to "play dead."

In morbid frames of mind, I've found, that unintended mimicry cuts too close to the bone. I feel distressed by the recognition that the familiar parts of me—my hardworking feet, for example, for which I feel a kind of forlorn pity since they bear the long scars of orthopedic operations I had as a child that seemed to do nothing but weaken them—carry within them the imminence of decay.

An obvious but saddening recognition. I have to get out of bed and walk around to shake off the sorrow it brings.

Sometimes I feel a childish wish to go on forever—an almost pathetic longing to be able to see the world after I've had to leave it. Even though I know that the sight—the passage of my children through time, for one—would break my heart.

So I try to cultivate what the poet John Keats, who was to die at twenty-five, proposed in a now-famous letter to his brothers in 1817.

Praising the genius of Shakespeare, he wrote of a quality he called "negative capability": a state of living in uncertainty, mystification, and receptivity that allows us to deeply imagine the perspectives of others.

Through this negative capability, he wrote, we're able to disappear enough that we can see ourselves as existing also in our fellows—inhabiting not only the finite moments and details of our own personhood, but the imagined personhood of others.

Keats was discussing the capacities and choices of writers, and his idea was specific to people. But I like to see it in more general terms, as a gesture that can extend beyond the bounds of the human into the realm of the beasts. And the green. Into a pantheism or animism of being that precludes no form of feeling.

I work on this, when I can. Try to project my imagination into the selves that are unlike mine.

And feel grateful that, for now, I get to be alive.

THE PRIVACY OF the mind gives us freedom, but at the price of a piercing aloneness.

There's a paperback on my shelf that I bought at a place called the Museum of Jurassic Technology in LA's Culver City. My favorite part of the book is the title, which marries arrogant bluster with a melancholy solitude: *No One May Ever Have the Same Knowledge Again.*

The individuality we hold so dear comes with a powerful sense of isolation that can bring on sadness and fear. It lurks waiting for us in the awareness of our personalities' confinement—the realization that our particular flashes of insight or delight, nuances of thinking and feeling, are locked into ourselves.

And finally, can't be shared.

We're understood by others not through our internal lives but through our external gestures, not by our thoughts but by our behavior and the subset of behavior that emerges as language. (Though some linguists argue that it's the other way around, that behavior is a subset of language.) But neither of those outward demonstrations is fully or exactly who each of us *is*. The ways of perceiving and being that are *us* are known only to us: we exist, and then cease to exist, essentially unknown.

And most of us don't wish for full exposure. The privacy of our thoughts is the most essential refuge we possess. To have our mental processes laid open—in all their microscopic suspicions, hostilities, and petty envies, all their wants and biases and small or large perversions— would be a nightmare.

Our minds are encoded into the architecture of our brains, nerves, blood vessels, and bones. But we still tend to see our minds and bodies as separate from each other. Partly this two-part picture of selfhood, articulated by Descartes in the 1600s, persists in our way of thinking because it gives us permission to see the body as a temporary vessel and the mind as its priceless content.

If the mind isn't *only* the matter of the body, then it may be able to outlive that body, existing beyond its confines. If the mind contains the soul, and the soul is eternal, dualism becomes a precondition of life after death.

And intuitively, the fact that our minds are self-aware—and able to perceive our bodies much as they perceive the rest of the world "outside" the brain—feels like proof of the mind's autonomy.

So the idea that, instead, the body is self-aware and the mind simply a part of it poses a threat to our exceptionalism as well as our shot at immortality.

For if our bodies are aware of themselves, so may other bodies be: the bodies of those who are not us.

Instead of an orderly hierarchy over which we preside, supreme in the spectatorship of our superior minds, the living world might be seen as an efflorescence of subjectivity: a soaring tree of experience, like Yggdrasil in Norse mythology. Among whose roots and branches and leaves all manner of creatures dwell.

Seeing the universe through billions of different eyes, hearing it through billions of different ears, feeling and tasting it through countless other sensory means.

So that the universe actually exists in as many forms as there are ways of knowing it—a multiverse not of theoretical physics but of perception. In postcolonial studies, this notion is applied to human cultures and thoughtways and referred to as the "pluriverse."

But outside the bounds of the human, a still greater pluriverse extends: a pluriverse of being that hovers around us all the time, brimming with mysteries.

And hidden from our view.

EVEN AS MY life depends on the inflow and outflow of molecules around me, I cling to a useful illusion of separateness. To focus on the constant precariousness of the many exchanges between the outside and inside, which lie beyond my conscious control—not only air and water and food and light, but viruses and bacteria and even the social contagion of fright or rage or other feelings that get transferred among people— would overwhelm me.

The fixed idea of our bodies' separation from the outside serves a survival drive, since we're regularly called upon to protect *us* from *not-us* in a world that presents an unending series of obstacles.

It's an easy instinct to put both the mind and the body in their boxes: the mind inside the box of the body, the body inside the boxes of the built world.

As boxes and frames multiply in our space and define our time, as we capture and contain ourselves within them and direct our attention toward their contents, we see and hear, more and more, imitations of life. In our frames, orderly simulations replace the more haphazard experience of real events.

In our captivation of looking at flat surfaces and listening to digital sound, increasingly we neglect the other senses.

Smell recedes, and with it the richness of a constant access to sensory memory—the scents of beloved people, of strangers and of crowds, of skin and place and bloom and rain, of food and fear and the synesthetic coolness of breathing in eucalyptus or peppermint.

Touch recedes, and with it the variety of textures and gestures and electricity we need to connect us with otherness—the three dimensions of our movement through space, the exposure of our nerve endings to old and new stimuli alike.

Those forms of feeling and communion that can only occur outside the boxes and frames begin to fade.

MAYBE IT'S THE permeability we work so hard to deny that accounts for the hopeful notions of mental control that drift at the margins of our imaginations. Precognition, say. Telepathy. Telekinesis.

In superhero fantasies—a story form whose appeal, since the first modern superheroes appeared in comic books shortly before the Second World War, has rarely dimmed—impossibly powerful men, and a few women, command abilities that lie outside the purview of the human. These include superspeed. Superstrength. Invisibility. X-ray vision. Heat-ray vision. Time travel. Astral projection.

Also, the underwater breathing that fish do. The flight of birds. The spontaneous regeneration of skin or limbs. Shape-shifting. Invincibility.

Once, in the stories we told of our origins, such transformations were miracles wrought by the gods. Or God. Now they're abilities vested in people through the interventions of science and technology.

The superheroes reflect and mimic the beasts, like hybrid deities. Stripped of divine origination and vested, instead, with powers given them by human inventiveness.

Those powers make them godlike—a guy I knew slightly in college, a handsome actor, went on to play Dr. Manhattan in the movie from the graphic novel series *Watchmen*. A massive, translucent naked white man, immortal and clairvoyant.

So rendered, in a direct inversion of the actual effects of nuclear fall-out on the human body, by radioactivity.

Superheroes are a product of the works of Man.

AS MAMMALS WE stay in one form from birth till death—we grow larger and stronger, then weaker again. But we always have the same body, though it replaces its cells constantly and suffers the subtractions and alterations of aging and injury. More and more we manipulate the details of our physiques through surgery or other means, but despite these modifications the bodies we inhabit remain the ones we were born with.

This isn't true of all the animals. Insects take many forms throughout their lives, and the different stages of their development, called instars, may be so different from each other that, without pictures to refer to, we'd never peg them as variations of the same individual.

Conenose kissing bugs, for example, have many instars, but only one

I can identify with confidence: the adult version, with a long black body edged in thin lines of crimson. Most times, when my boyfriend or I find an insect or arachnid in the house—usually wolf spiders or bark scorpions—we slide it into a cup and take it outside. But I kill conenose kissing bugs as soon as I see them, since they're bloodsuckers and can carry a nasty disease called Chagas, and since their bites raise ugly welts on my daughter's skin and large, purple lumps on my mother, who has an allergy.

By the time I recognize them, they're often already fattened with our blood.

A butterfly or moth hardly resembles its caterpillar incarnation. Mollusks, like clams, drift through the water as larvae, sometimes for months, before settling on a hard surface, filtering calcium out of the water, and using it to build their shells and assume their mature forms.

Numerous species of reptiles and amphibians can grow new tails. Curious salamanders called axolotls are able to produce anew not only missing limbs and tails, but also more vital, central components—parts of their brains and spinal cords, ovaries, and lungs.

Native only to the area around Mexico City, whose canals are their last remaining habitat outside captivity, axolotls don't metamorphose into terrestrial forms, as many other salamanders do, but spend their whole lives in water.

Their ability to regrow body parts throughout their lives has made them the focus of numerous scientific efforts to identify the cellular mechanisms at work. The hope is that one day such mechanisms might be applied to human limb regeneration. An axolotl's "skin, bone, cartilage, and muscle can be regrown many times with no sign of trauma," although experiments involving repeated choppings-off of their legs have shown that by the fifth amputation of the "same" leg, regrowth is only partial.

In appearance the axolotl is both weird and cute. The frilly pink or purple gill plumes that branch out from the sides of its neck make it look part plant or part coral. It has a pale body, dark, widely spaced eyes, and a mouth shaped into a permanent, shy, sweet-seeming smile.

Some species of planarian flatworms can be decapitated and grow new heads. Back in 1898 scientists showed they could regenerate from a fragment as small as *one-279th* the size of the original self. And then, in the 1960s, other scientists demonstrated these water-living worms could learn a task, have their heads amputated, regenerate a head from the tail section, and still perform the task. Even without their heads, they had retained learned information.

Aspersions were later cast on the methods of those experiments, but more recent studies have supported their findings.

One example, possibly, of an intelligence of the body.

A CREATURE CALLED the immortal jellyfish, *Turritopsis dohrnii*, is capable of reverting to a sexually immature stage after reaching full maturity. And beginning life again. The subject of much research on aging, it has spread all over from its origins in the Pacific. Likely in ballast water, which is how many invasive saltwater species travel from one part of the global ocean to another.

Immortal jellies are steadily achieving what one marine scientist has called a "worldwide silent invasion."

They have recent exposure in pop culture: they're known to avid YouTube watchers like my son.

What if you turned into a baby again, one day, he said to me in the car one morning. Driving to school.

Like that jellyfish, he said. How terrible it would be. For us. To be an immortal.

The beasts regenerate themselves and rise again.

9

IN THE EIGHTIES Sony Walkmans were everywhere. Their pocket-sized cassette player/radios allowed you to stroll through public places in a private musical setting. Just like that, the commonplace—your humdrum passage through well-known daily spaces—could be transformed into a movie. Because wherever you went and whatever you were doing could be scored by a customized soundtrack.

Before the Walkman, in the days of the home stereo, music had typically been a shared social experience. Not anymore.

I forged my way along subway platforms and city streets with the Walkman in my coat pocket and earphones on, listening to pop and rock and opera highlights and daydreaming. I took the subway to school every day, from the age of twelve on, and rarely did so unaccompanied by music. The songs I chose scribed even the most routine of forward motion into a personal journey—a thrilling vector that gave me slow tempos and fast. Breathtaking swells and melancholy pauses, charged pulses of adrenaline, heart-clutching moments of longing.

No one else knew any of it. They didn't know the brimming euphoria that poured forth from that musical score. Had no inkling, as I passed them on the street, of the impassioned soundscape that encapsulated—from my perspective—all of us. How it cast other people into a vivid dramatic relief.

And made them into walk-ons in the story of me.

Looking back, I can see that story was a romance—not one of the cheap Harlequins I liked to read and mock back then, not a tale of how a princess won a prince, but an epic of individuality. Life was the setting for a drama of self-realization. And though the story was lacking, I have no doubt, in both humility and empathy, maybe that solipsistic drive allowed for greater ecstasy. Maybe my barely nascent access to fellow feeling—along with rushes of hormones and a neural circuitry arranged to respond to new stimuli with a surge of energy and pleasure—made for a rapturous availability to social experience. To other people as a source of sensory and imaginative delight.

Connected to the ability to give and receive delight, and also to withhold it, was a magnetic awareness of the self as a locus of power. A self that could command a secret dominion of events and emotions beyond the family and old familiar friends.

The story invited me to project onto less familiar objects—new crushes and boyfriends, charismatic young teachers, even distant pop stars and actors—an idea of my own ascendant personhood as I tried to see myself through their eyes. Of my face and gestures and styles in relation to theirs.

It inspired the construction of a mental romance between myself, the subject, and—as Roland Barthes suggested in *A Lover's Discourse*—my image in the mirror.

As I read it, anyway, in Barthes's conception of the idolization of this mirror image, the primary dynamic is between a self and its self-vision. So that any love object is a third party to this vision: a triangulator. Almost an incidental addition.

Seen through that lens, our romances with partners—anointed by the culture as the central social narrative of our lives—can be more clearly understood as an ongoing romance with our image of ourselves.

A form of self-worship dressed up as the adoration of another.

I HAD MANY boyfriends as a teenager, so varied in personality and interests that now I see little commonality among them.

There was a guy with a babyish face I dated for a whole year, at the age of thirteen, who would later throw a party to celebrate his first million. There was a track star who was always more in love with a beautiful friend of mine than with me and went on to work for a manufacturer of athletic shoes. For almost forty years after high school I never saw or spoke to this fast runner, but then he came to Arizona for the Super Bowl in 2023, when I met him for dinner and was delighted by his candor and intelligence. There was a gruff but warmhearted suburban jock who would eventually work in finance in London; there was a Marxist graduate student I met at the university library, bespectacled and mild-seeming but with abusive tendencies, who would die shortly after we broke up in a US-sponsored bombing in Central America, where he was helping Sandinista rebels to build a school.

There was a kind boy I met in West Berlin who was part Native American and went on to become a lawyer for the tribes in California; a rich Frenchman I knew on the coast of Spain who danced in the local discos every night, tried and failed to teach me windsurfing, and believed in the virtues of the rhythm method. There was a trainee for the German Secret Service who, in the aftermath of 9/11, would be detailed to a high-profile investigation of Khalid Sheikh Mohammed and in 2018 took my daughter and me on a driving tour of castles and Holocaust sites; there was a quiet Norwegian whose family owned a chain of jewelry shops.

In college there was a frustrated fraternity bro whose last name I've forgotten and whom I've therefore never been able to stalk on the internet; a talented Anglo-Argentine actor who eventually became an international expert on oak trees and is still my friend; a drug dealer from the depressing London exurb of Wokingham who barely noticed my presence, smoked hashish constantly, and passed his weekends in a daze watching sculling on the Thames; a very tall, white architect from Princeton, dedicated to spreading the gospel of the blues, who made me mixtapes of Howlin' Wolf and Screamin' Jay Hawkins.

The only thing the disparate boyfriends shared was good looks.

I spent a lot of time and effort on the drama and intrigue of dating them—constructing romance after romance in which those handsome boyfriends reflected the glory of me.

FOR EARLY HUMANS, mirrors were pools of unmoving water that couldn't have furnished much detail. Possibly a boon, since early human grooming probably focused on parasite removal. Along with hair management, also related to parasites. Neanderthals used shells as tweezers for plucking hair, and cave paintings show men without beards from twenty thousand years ago, though some may have been naturally hairless. But the plucking and shaving was likely often cooperative rather than self-administered, and gazing at a watery reflection less compelling than hunting down ground sloths and competing with cave hyenas.

Around eight thousand years ago, mirrors were fashioned of obsidian, a black glass created by volcanoes. Next came polished copper or stone, then bronze.

The Bronze Age ended around 1200 BC, when its empire of trade stretching from Egypt to Afghanistan broke down abruptly due to widespread drought, famine, earthquakes, and waves of invaders known as the "sea people," who were probably refugees. The tin needed for bronze came from Afghanistan, while the silver the empire traded in came from Greece and the gold from Nubia and Sudan. When trade between them ceased, so did the dominance of bronze.

Out of the ashes of that collapsed civilization arose the Iron Age, when Phoenicians—from whom we inherited the Greek alphabet—sailed the Mediterranean.

Not long after the birth of Christ, the first mirrors were made with coatings of metal behind glass.

Ancient mirrors produced distorted images. *We saw through a glass darkly*, as Corinthians says, *but then face to face . . .* As detail improved, mirrors began to appoint the rooms of princes and merchants. And were eventually manufactured in bulk.

Now, in our businesses and homes and on our streets, reflective surfaces are everywhere we look. We can't avoid their reproductions of ourselves. Even when we want to.

But fewer and fewer of us seem to want to—the young, more than the old, seek mirrors all the time. Their phones are mirrors and the internet is mirrors. All halls are halls of mirrors.

Mirrors define the real, and the real is the reflected self.

THOSE GROUND SLOTHS that we used to hunt, when we were unmirrored Early Man, have passed into oblivion. The sloths we know now are famously slow-moving and even adopted as pets: one 1960s family wrote a book about their pet sloth called *A Sloth in the Family* that tells how the animal once fell asleep while draped over a lampshade. And didn't bother to wake up when they discovered its fur was burning.

But the now-extinct ground sloths, of which there were many species, were massive, with fearsome claws. Because they were big enough to swallow avocados whole, they were key vectors in the dispersal of these now-beloved fruits. Their presence in the fossil records of the Americas dates back about 35 million years—the last to live on the continents' mainland were possibly hunted into memory by humans a little over ten thousand years ago.

Cave hyenas seem to have competed with Neanderthals for hospitable home sites, and also to have been killed and butchered by them. Hyenas ranged across Eurasia, from modern-day Spain to Siberia; large populations in the far east of Russia may have helped delay human colonization of North America.

But they died out some twelve thousand years back, at the end of that Ice Age, along with other northern megafauna.

Not long after people and their wolf dogs reached Alaska.

Instead of cave hyenas we have spotted hyenas, now, who live in Africa. These were first thought by Europeans—including writers like Ernest Hemingway—to be hermaphrodites.

Hemingway, often touted as a master of restrained and minimalist language, referred to the hyena in "The Snows of Kilimanjaro" as a "hermaphroditic, self-eating devourer of the dead."

The misconception may have derived from the fact that the females have a "pseudo-penis," also known as a penile clitoris, that closely resembles an actual penis. It even appears to have testicles—external labia fused together in a way that makes them look like a scrotum. The penile clitoris can become erect, rounding off the completeness of the illusion. Female spotted hyenas give birth through this structure, and its susceptibility to tearing means first-time mothers suffer from unusually high mortality.

Hyenas are often vilified, as in *The Lion King*, where they're portrayed as evil thieves.

In fact they're good hunters as well as accomplished scavengers. They live in matriarchal clans and have faces as soulful and intelligent as any other creature's—see, for instance, Joel Sartore's Photo Ark, in which animals are memorialized.

MYSELF, I WASN'T RAISED with access to wilderness. The outdoors, sure, but always within shouting distance of a building.

My father was a dedicated city person who wished to be near public transit—since he didn't have a driver's license—and academic libraries. So we never went hiking or camping: I don't remember a single hike or night in a tent. Unless you count the large tepee, modeled on those of the Plains Indians, that he constructed for us in the backyard.

But on camping trips I've made as an adult, in those rare days away from mirrors, I've realized how frequently, in regular life, I must check myself in them.

Out in the woods or the desert, with no precise reflective surface to gaze into, my face recedes from my awareness. Even my social presence feels like it's fading away—as though, without constant reminders of how I look to others, I'm losing my hold on the details of my separate identity.

When mirrors are absent, we see other people's faces instead of our own.

Our mirrored selves are flipped horizontally, which we can check easily by holding up a piece of text that comes out reversed: mirrors turn words into glyphs. But the notion that mirror images are backward somehow puzzles us, even when we know it rationally. Objects look different reversed, yet we find this hard to remember when it applies to our own faces—the fact that every adjustment we make daily, in front of the mirror, is the product of a horizontal illusion.

I've always felt I look better in mirrors than in photos. Whenever I have to look at a photograph of myself instead of a mirror image, it feels like my familiar home has just turned out to be a hovel.

INCREASINGLY WE WATCH without being seen.

When we decide to put ourselves on display—as in social media, into whose frames we place numerous pictures of our faces—we give out simulations, filtered and lit to remove blemishes. Competitive in their drive to attain a perfection that, strictly speaking, is not human.

The frames, like our boxes of space and time, are such mainstays of our physical and cognitive spaces that by the turn of the twenty-first century they'd become an organizing principle. Windows are everywhere, but rather than offering us a view of a wide, often frightening, and certainly diverse landscape, they mostly show us fictionalized versions of each other. The content we stream is mainly images of people.

Plus pets, commanding millions of followers, whose adorability augments and represents our own while simultaneously occurring in a safe and separate compartment.

When a landscape does appear in our frames, it's likely to be as an idealized form of scenery—an enviable backdrop to our leisure activities. Shots of idyllic vacation spots. Aquamarine waters, white-sand beaches.

More typically the frames are filled by those similar to us. White people if we're white. Rich people if we're rich. Right-wing people if we're right-wing, left if we're left. Communities selling themselves to themselves, so that the frames direct our gaze inward.

Most of our little windows never open.

I look at my daughter and son, with their several devices, friend circles and music and miniature theaters, meme culture and gaming culture, Instagram influencers and YouTube celebrities. All chosen by or for them. And come to see my old Walkman as the modest dawn of the tailored worldscape they inhabit now. Since I could shape the mood and texture and words of my passage through space and time as they do, though less constantly and only in one dimension; since the real and the present could be easily overlaid and transformed by a familiar playlist.

My Walkman was an early filter, a bulwark against the outside. Communal music didn't disappear—we still went to concerts, still went to dances, still played songs in our houses with friends—but there was now a private stream that could erase, in almost any context, the ambient sounds of place, of traffic and birds and other people.

In the filter economy, which through its infinite variations on a theme disguises sameness as newness, the stream of stimuli my kids receive is a repeated iteration of their previous selections—their former tastes and selves are constantly affirmed. As everyone's are. Except that with them the streamlining of self into self, identity group into identity group— same into same—has occurred at such an early age that otherness barely stands a chance.

MORE AND MORE, it seems to me, human parents are like an octopus.

Male octopuses can be distinguished from female, to the human eye, chiefly by a groove in one of their arms. They mate in a way that, to me, seems courtly: a male reaches out an arm to a female, and if she accepts it, passes along a packet of sperm.

Females reproduce only once—though a certain species has been found, at unusual depth and coldness in the ocean off California, that seems to violate this rule—with a brood of eggs the female protects from predators with her body before they disperse as larvae. That dispersal is soon followed by her death.

For highly intelligent animals, octopuses have very short lives—only one to two years on average. Along with their reproductive strategies, this means they can't hand down their lifeways or their history: an octopus never knows her or his children, except as eggs. She releases the eggs into the water, then dies. Tells her babies no tales, imparts no culture, dispenses no lessons in how to get by.

This is true of many animals—fishes and other mollusks among them—but not of any animals whose neurological processes appear to be as complex as those of the octopus.

Each individual takes its abilities and knowledge to the grave. The new generation starts once again at zero, left to the currents and the predators. In an eternal cycle of reset.

10

THE ILLUMINATED MANUSCRIPTS known as bestiaries—collections of images of animals along with descriptions or parables—flourished in medieval Europe. They followed an earlier Christian prototype, the *Physiologus* of ancient Greece that dated from a century or two AD and was still circulated in the Middle Ages. But also the animal morality tales of *Aesop's Fables* some eight hundred years before that—oral stories told in Greece around 600 BC.

Those fables were only compiled in writing about three centuries later, and it's not clear whether Aesop was an actual person—likely a slave—or a conflation of sources or both. Now the animal tales ascribed to him are treated as children's fare, but at the time they were for all age groups and mixed in with the lurid exploits of people and gods.

Bestiaries sometimes included minerals as well as animals and plants. They didn't usually distinguish between actual beasts and imaginary ones, as their authors either weren't sure or didn't much care whether a creature they were describing lived out there somewhere, in the real world, or only in legend. And their vivid illustrations and tales of beasts, from hedgehogs to owls and phoenixes, often had little to do with the animals to which they referred, even when those animals were real ones.

Pelicans, for example, were typically painted blue, with short, sharp beaks like a raptor's, by illuminators who'd never seen them. As surely as they'd never seen a phoenix or a unicorn.

These seabirds were symbols of Christ, the bestiaries said, because the mother birds pierced their own breast and fed their young with the blood. As Christ had shed his own blood for the faithful.

Some of those images are still floating around, buried in everyday and symbolic life: a bleeding pelican adorns the state flag of Louisiana.

When gems and minerals had their own dedicated manuscripts, those were known as lapidaries, while compendia of plants—dietary and curative—were called herbals.

Hildegard of Bingen, a healer and visionary who lived in the twelfth century and was later made a saint, wrote an herbal called *Physica*, a thick reference work enumerating the qualities and uses of medicinal and edible plants that's still being reprinted. She's considered by some to have been the founder of the study of natural history in Europe.

Another prodigious German scholar, a Dominican friar of the thirteenth century named Albertus Magnus, set himself the monumental task of studying and commenting on all of Aristotle's works. The goal was to reconcile them with his Catholic faith. He produced all three of the encyclopedic varieties—bestiaries, lapidaries, and herbals—and like Hildegard would be canonized. He had Thomas Aquinas as a student, founded a university, and during his time as a bishop reputedly insisted on going everywhere on foot.

To sit astride an animal would have violated the vows of humility of his monastic order.

IN THE HEYDAY of the bestiary—before the European conquest of the far corners of the globe, before the Industrial Revolution and the rise of fossil fuels, and before market capitalism came to define our social and economic behavior—the animals and plants were God's children.

They may not have had the exact same souls we did, may not have been shaped in the same image of the Lord, but they were his creation. And he saw that they were good.

In numerous Bible verses, it was advised to treat the other animals with tenderness. *A righteous man regardeth the life of his beasts*, cautions

Proverbs. *If you see the donkey of one who hates you lying down under its burden,* says Exodus, *you shall rescue it with him.*

The splendor of nature, in bestiaries, was seen as the word of God; the beasts were expressions of that word.

I USE THE TERM *beast* not in debasement but with reverence, to honor the exquisite strangeness of the other animals.

In the past we've called some of them brutes, freaks, fiends, and even demons. At times we still do. But the beasts are only the rich host of the living beyond us.

Some we relate to easily, while others are beyond the range of our ready empathy. The beastliness of the beasts is as variable as their forms.

Likewise the plants and trees and all that lives greenly—the realm of the green, too, contains multitudes.

An array of wonders that surpasses understanding.

IN THE PAST, as we went about the business of living, the others were always presumed to be there. We knew the faces and sounds of some, from the trees and scrub, from our gardens and farms. The rivers and oceans we fished in, the beaches we walked along. We knew the forms and movements of those we saw farther distant—the flocks in the sky, the herds on the grasslands, the schools moving through water.

Their essences were ambient in the world. We understood the places we lived in by the others that lived there too, enmeshed in our rhythms as surely as the passing of days from dawn to dusk, the face of the moon emerging from clouds.

Our reliance on the others seldom needed to be stated, as we evolved together over the fathomless span of time.

It was a precondition.

Our coexistence has been, since forever, the backdrop of being. A dappled, shifting impression like the patterns of sun and shadows that fall across beds and ceilings and walls, maybe—a togetherness we've perceived as always already there, and so, at times, hardly perceived at all.

But still depend on, as we depend on each other.

Say, the way our streets can turn to velvet at night, and the lit-up windows of other houses signal to us in the gloaming—the unknown, intimate worlds of our neighbors, bringing us comfort by their presence alone. The way a faint music, drifting over the air between apartment buildings in a city block, reminds us of the private lives of its listeners. Never to be our friends, maybe, but linked to us by the strains of a familiar melody.

Or the way the dull roar of a lawn mower wakes us on a slow morning and the smell of cut grass takes us, in a second, back to childhood. Evoking the nostalgia of a barely remembered moment.

Maybe we haven't spoken up for the others partly because of the unconscious, innate quality of our ties with them.

Possibly we need the telescopic view—the distance of forgetting and the jolt of recognition as a remembrance surfaces—to know what we adore.

Maybe we can only look back in longing, over time or space, when the object of our care is far away.

And our old home is gone.

OVER THE PAST half-century the planet's wildlife populations have declined by an average of 69 percent.

In Central and South America the decline has been closer to 94 percent, if the figures reported in a World Wildlife Fund study from 2022 are accurate.

The primary driver of this breathtaking disappearance, according to the scientists who authored the report, has been habitat loss and degradation. Mainly for the production of human food.

Some say we're eating up the world.

IN A DREAM I had there's a girl on a path through some trees. Dark trunks soar up around her into a cloud of green.

It's my own mother, turned young again. From a time before she had me, when everything lay open and nothing had been decided.

She doesn't look like my mother used to, in the old photos I've seen, but I know it's her anyway. That's how it is, in dreams.

She tells me the city is gray. She doesn't like it anymore. It's fast and sharp and has too many corners.

There's something we forgot, she says. A place where everything is curved. I'm going back. Walk in the woods with me.

They've built a little bridge across a stream.

Where are we *going*? I ask.

Whining a bit, maybe.

Over the creeks and springs, over the rocks and moss. Beneath the shade. Come on! she says. You're so *slow*.

My mother can be stern.

I'm *tired*, I say.

Wait—she looks younger. She's even younger than I am.

But that can't be.

Is this a fairy tale? I ask.

She doesn't answer.

Is it a story where the animals can talk? I still like those stories. Where the animals can talk.

Well, they don't *talk*, she says. But they can sing.

She doesn't say this to me directly. It's on her back, somehow. Like a shimmering bruise.

There's music in the dark. We reach a clearing in the pines. Oh: that's what this is. A party!

I recognize it from the music and the strings of twinkling lights.

Or are they fireflies? I'm not sure.

People are dancing. I'm glad. I haven't been to a party in so long. No one ever wants to dance with me these days. I have to do it alone in my room. If not, the children get embarrassed. And say my music is too loud.

Looking out at the crowd in its festivities, still hesitating in the black and green of trees, I notice some of the people are bears. There's a guy who could be a buffalo. On a table a few sparrows are strutting around. Small but crotchety, as if they own the place.

There's an alligator with snaggleteeth, but he's friendly. He's from a picture book my mother used to read to me, where he saved a town from flooding. His name is Alexander.

There's even a badger. With stripes on his face.

Where is the singing coming from? Oh, I see—a tall white bird with a long neck. She has two wings stretched down beside her like a wedding dress.

The song is sad, but you can dance to it.

Then I begin to feel nervous. The little girl's walking away, toward the crowd. She's confident.

The small mother is leaving me behind.

But wait, I beg her. Wait for me. I don't *know* anyone.

Of course you do, she says. They've always been your friends.

MINE EYES HAVE SEEN THE GLORY

1

RETURNING FROM A work trip one time, our father brought us puzzling gifts—three rabbits' feet on key chains, one for each of us, in three different colors. White, gray-brown, and black.

We had no keys to put on the chains, but that didn't matter, he said. They were for rubbing when we had a wish or a worry. They were good-luck charms.

He was a softhearted man who liked animals very much, in general, and we trusted that he didn't mean them any harm. So we tried to be grateful for the gifts. Still, he saw the dismay in our faces and did his best to reassure us: the rabbits hadn't been killed for their feet.

His disclaimer confused us.

When we stroked the soft fur of those disembodied paws, it was not to bring us luck but in an act of contrition. We wanted to show those absent rabbits—hopping along sadly, somewhere, on their three remaining feet—how very sorry we were.

HE WAS AN EGYPTOLOGIST, my father, and kept an array of artifacts and replicas in his basement study. Among them were statuettes of Bast, the ancient Egyptian cat god, and a stone figure of Babi the baboon god.

Babi was the deification of hamadryas baboons, a species known for its pink buttocks and the harem structure of its family groups, which primatologists call OMUs, or "one-male units." OMUs are dominated by a male who mates with several females.

As a virile god, Babi was often pictured with a prominent and—to the modern eye, anyway—comical erection.

Thoth, the god of magic and wisdom, was also partial to baboons and was sometimes represented with a baboon head. Other times he had the head of an ibis, a wading bird with a long, curved bill.

The ancient Egyptians bred cats, dogs, and crocodiles purely for ceremonial use and caught vast numbers of wild sacred ibises for the purpose of sacrifice. Thoth received dead ibises in staggering volume. No fewer than four million of the mummified birds have been found at a site called Tuna el-Gebel, and nearly two million at the burial grounds of Saqqara.

There are no sacred ibises in Egypt anymore.

People worshipped an extensive cast of characters back then, some animal, some part animal, and some human: the gods were multiple and multiform.

During the empires of Greece and Rome they took the shape of men and women, though bigger, stronger, and more beautiful. But these gods were changeable and still closely interwoven with the world of the beasts. Many could morph into animals at will—Zeus became a swan and an eagle and a bull. Humans were turned into other beings by the gods: Daphne into a tree, Narcissus into a white flower, Arachne the weaver into the first spider.

Eventually the Roman Empire helped Christianize continental Europe, where, to my own forebears, there was increasingly only one god. And although he was sometimes represented by an animal, say a lamb or a lion or a fish—although he was born among animals and dwelt in harmony with them—he never changed into one. He never crossed the beastly boundary. The only part of him that was not human was his godhood, an invisible and divine flame.

Christ had a human face. Echoed in mirror images of our own.

JESUS WASN'T WHITE, I heard a historian say on public radio. Wouldn't have had blue eyes. Rather, the son of God most likely had black hair. Brown eyes. Olive-brown skin. That was how guys looked in ancient Judea.

No one described him as handsome in the Bible, either, unlike Moses. The New Testament, this scholar said, contains no physical description of Jesus before his death—only after the Resurrection, when he was trans-figured. And his face shone like the sun.

Many early reports, even into the sixth century, suggested that Christ was abject, infirm, and small and crooked in his body, with some authors pegging his height at three cubits: four foot six. In these now-apocryphal accounts he was a suffering servant, as prophesied in Isaiah. One of the earliest possible images of Jesus, from Syria around 235 AD—a ver-sion of "The Healing of the Paralytic"—seems to show a beardless and short-haired man.

But Church Fathers like Saint Augustine, in the fourth century, insisted Christ must have been ideal in face and form. Nothing less than physical perfection would have befitted the son of God.

By the Middle Ages, European artists were painting him as a thin, white man of radiant handsomeness. The long hair they frequently gave him, rendering his appearance softer and more feminine, was also a creative choice, possibly made to distinguish his figure from those of other men. Paul the Apostle, who knew Jesus and some of his family, described long hair on a man, in 1 Corinthians, as "a shame unto him." Which he might not have written had the man himself sported long, flowing locks.

This redesign of God wasn't trivial in the stories told about him. Visual art was what brought narrative to the masses—particularly in times and places where the spoken languages weren't the same as the written ones, and when many people could not or did not read. And this is still the case, only now our images move.

By the nineteenth century, it was being suggested in some European circles, and by American eugenicists like Madison Grant, that Jesus had looked Aryan. Sometimes Nordic—sometimes a blond.

In their paintings and sculptures, the Europeans had recast God in their own likeness.

BETWEEN THE FIFTEENTH CENTURY and the present day, the countries of Europe undertook a series of colonization schemes—projections, out of those proud nations where men looked so much like their god, of a godlike power.

The Chinese had invented gunpowder—a mixture of potassium nitrate, sulfur, and charcoal—hundreds of years before: ninth-century Taoist monks who were searching for the elixir of youth. China was using petroleum as a fuel as early as the fourth century BC, and Japan by the seventh century AD: in this technology, as well, Asia was far ahead of the Western curve.

It took about four centuries for gunpowder to reach the West, and centuries more for it to become a dominant force. With its assistance, and with that of coal and timber and oil, European nations secured trade routes by force, founding far-flung empires of nature plunder. Their scholars produced writings, still solemnly invoked by modern economists, that said the best way to attain prosperity was to do what you wished, in trade, with as few constraints as possible.

If you were a white, Christian man and belonged to a nation of same.

This was the "free" market or "free" trade, where freedom equated with the satisfaction of desire. Which economists prefer to call demand.

Meanwhile Western people were becoming more subject to laws that replaced local, traditional, and informal agreements as common law was replaced by laws codified in writing. Against the theft of property. Against assault and murder and, much later, rape, though marital rape and various forms of murder remain legal in a few places now. The content of written laws has always been controversial: in France, as the writer Emmanuel Carrère reported in *Lives Other Than My Own*, some say criminal law is a tool to stop the poor from stealing from the rich. While civil law is a tool that allows the rich to steal from the poor.

And much as crimes among persons were regulated and penalized, governments, too, were increasingly bound by a stricture of rules.

But corporations and their assigns have always commanded a special status, since the global market, whose redoubt extends beyond and between the borders of defined regional and national power centers, operates in a fuzzier rule-space that persists today: the United Nations casts only a frail and pale shadow. International laws remain far weaker and less enforceable than laws within nations, and many of the most powerful privateers of the market continue to occupy a no-man's-land between and outside legal systems.

As I write, for example, the entire seabed of the global ocean—and the ability to allow its destruction through mining—is governed from a tiny, less-than-transparent office with a small staff, located in Jamaica, called the International Seabed Authority.

Often, as it functions in the gray zones of territoriality, the market has been able to shrug off the inconvenient burdens of both legality and morality in favor of what it calls "efficiency." Historically, when companies thieved—say from a tribe or newly colonized nation—they claimed they were merely taking ownership of what was rightfully theirs. With the approval of their sponsor governments.

When the companies or their agents committed genocides against native peoples, they were simply defending their property. When market hunters descended on the vast, living bestiaries of the Great Plains—the American Serengeti, as the historian and author Dan Flores has called it—they turned 15 million delicate, gazelle-like pronghorns into a few thousand, and 30 million towering bison into a few hundred.

But they were just using the land. And the creatures and plants that lived there.

In those majestic plains the abundance of herds and flocks was once so glorious and sublime a spectacle that European explorers marveled at the sight, comparing it to Eden. But those who followed them denuded the plains of most of their animal life and left, in their wake, a plainer and emptier landscape we now dismiss as "flyover country."

HAVING ONLY ONE GOD is a form of efficiency, too, since multiple gods can be confusing. In the highly popular *Percy Jackson* books my children read and reread several times, the rivalries of the ancient Greek gods are fictionalized in a modern setting for a youth readership. The hook is that demigods live among us and take the form of outcast teenagers: if you feel isolation and otherness, say because you have dyslexia like Percy, it may turn out you're a secret demigod.

In the old stories and the new, factions of deities demanded different offerings from their subjects and battled fiercely among themselves. You could easily anger one god while struggling to obey another.

Monotheism was a streamlining of the hierarchy, a simplification of the old multiplex of loyalties. In Christian countries the coupling of faith with monarchies, whose kings and queens governed by "divine right," cemented the alliance between single figureheads of state and single godheads of the church—though not without the occasional tussle over whether a king or a pope was closer to God.

Monopolies of supplies and exchange opened the door to monopolies of ideas, and the massive deployment of missionaries helped to ensure the lockstep march of both: natural-resource extraction and Christianity. Swiftly, in the short span of a couple of centuries, European Christians took over about four-fifths of the world and methodically stripped it of its forests and grasslands and beasts.

This is not to say that European Christians were the sole group that might have proved equal to the task. Only that they were the ones who performed it.

GLOBALLY POPULAR BOOK SERIES for young and middle readers, from *Narnia* to *Percy Jackson* and *Harry Potter* and Philip Pullman's *His*

Dark Materials, are all extravagantly populated by beasts, both mythical and real. Without their casts of glamorous animals these books would be divested of much of their colorful magic.

AS A KID I sometimes went to a service in a church or synagogue with grandparents or friends: my parents—who'd say they were agnostics or atheists, if you were so intrusive as to ask—thought the experiences might broaden my perspective.

I was supremely bored by the Protestant services, where there was nothing to look at. And no wafers to eat or wine to drink. The ones I was invited to weren't ecstatic or demonstrative but buttoned-up and staid.

Catholic services, with their dramatic stagecraft and elaborate rituals, were more interesting to me. Unlike Catholicism, Judaism and Islam prohibit the worshipping, and even the creation, of "graven images"— representational statues and possibly pictures, if you don't take *graven* to mean exclusively *carved.*

With the exception of Episcopal and Anglican denominations, which, thanks to the wife-killer king Henry VIII, are historically close to Catholicism and do feature colorful human figures in their stained-glass windows—most Protestant churches also see the ban on images as a divine directive. Hence the general absence, in its places of worship, of crucifixes and representational pictures.

The Catholic Church had been propagating icons and other glorifying art long before Martin Luther nailed his theses to a door, and without its love of visual pageantry we wouldn't have bestiaries, with their magnificent griffins and centaurs and unicorns. Or any other Catholic masterpieces.

Still, where humility is concerned—a core Christian value—the rule against graven images, in retrospect, starts to look pretty sound.

At least when it comes to the part where white men decided the son of God was also a white man. And forcibly converted people across the globe, who did not look like him, to a white-man-worshipping creed. Telling themselves, as they robbed those other peoples of their wealth, their culture, and their freedom, that they were doing them a favor. A *spiritual* favor: the saving of their souls.

Which faith assured them could not—absolutely could *not!* you see—be saved by any other means.

WHEN WE WERE LITTLE my father told us "talk stories" every night at bedtime, which he made up as he went along. These were often accompanied by delicate pen-and-ink drawings, and their subjects were children and animals. Sometimes the children were us.

It hurts me to remember how we became impatient and turned away from his talk stories, in retrospect so lovely.

When we got older he introduced us to the classics from his own boyhood. We could read them ourselves by then. Mostly they came from England. More rarely, the United States. Plus there were the fairy and folk tales of Europe. And the *Arabian Nights*.

His favorites among those stories, and ours too, were tales of speaking beasts who lived in magical kingdoms. In the best-known series we read, which I only found out years later was an allegory of Christianity, God took the shape of a noble, majestic lion with a flowing mane.

He was protective of children and ferocious to their enemies.

Instead of being converted to Christianity by the land of Narnia, though, we were converted to lion worship.

Such is the hazard of allegory.

Even now, when someone says "God," the image that comes to me first is the face of a lion.

2

MY PARENTS WEREN'T bent on their kids winning things—they weren't the tiger mother or the all-American sports dad. They expected us to do our homework, true, and supported our athletic and artistic efforts, but they weren't the types to chant our names with a zealous intensity from the bleachers. Or deliver pep talks on the need to rise above the rest.

Still, even by grade school—and even if you had mild-mannered and bookish parents—winning was cropping up all around. You could win at games, sports, and school. You could win on almost any field. Or lose. And obviously you should try to win.

We all *liked* to win. If you didn't win, at least sometimes, you started to seem like a loser. Carried around your loser status like a rock. What did you have besides your reputation?

But some kids *needed* to win. Miniature vectors of dominance. Tiresome, frankly.

I was one of those. In games and sports, back then, I was a sore loser. My sulks when I lost were so bleak that my neighborhood friends probably *let* me win, as my siblings sometimes did. To avoid the shared punishment of my bad mood—bitter remarks about the fairness of the contest. Excuses over the reasons for my loss.

To me, being a loser equated with vanishing.

And I preferred not to vanish. In the present *or* future. I'd barely been around for a decade when I began to fantasize about never dying. Barely lived on the earth for a moment when it started to seem to me, in private flights of feeling, that *this* small splinter of self, *this* here fragment of secret, childish spirit, should be allowed to go on. Into the realm of forever, where the heroes and saints also went. But I didn't want to be a saint, of course. Not a martyr, anyway.

And how would I pull off hero?

I didn't know why or how. Only that I never wished to be nothing.

I *will* not leave this place, I vowed. They'll never, ever make me. I'll find a way to stay.

AND DEATH SHALL *have no dominion*, wrote Dylan Thomas the drunkard poet. *Though they sink through the sea they shall rise again.*

Exactly, I'd think when I read the poem in high school. That's how I've always felt.

EVERY SATURDAY MORNING my father would take my brother and sister and me to a corner mini-mart we called the candy store. We'd walk there after we visited the local library—we didn't own a television, so we went through piles of library books each week.

Near the candy store lived a friend of my mother's. She and her husband, a minister who would later ascend the ranks in his church to become an archdeacon, had a daughter who was my friend. If I slept over on a weekend night, her parents would wake us at an early hour the next day. They'd strip our blankets off and sing:

Rise, and shine, and give God your glory glory, children, of the, Lord.

One time I'd slept over there on a Friday night and missed the library trip with my father, so after we rose and shone she and I walked to the candy store by ourselves.

We both had allowances to spend, I believed. Mine was forty-five cents. My siblings and I each got five cents a week, per year of life.

At the store I found myself ten cents short of being able to purchase a coveted packet of sour chewing gum.

Chewing gum was outlawed in my home—our parents smoked plenty of Player's Lights cigarettes and each drank two tumblers of rye whiskey before dinner, during what they called "drinking and talking time," but my father drew the line at gum.

A filthy habit. Not to be tolerated on any account.

I planned to stuff my cheeks with the delicious, mouth-puckering contraband as I walked home, then spit it into a neighbor's garbage can before I got there.

Less greedy than I was, my friend bought barely anything and offered to lend me ten cents of her own.

But when we got back to her house, her mother greeted us at the front door.

She eyed my paper bag of loot and seemed suspicious of me.

I got the sinking feeling that she always had been.

Right off the bat, she asked if her daughter still had all her communion money. For church the next morning.

My friend admitted her offering would be short, because she'd lent some of it to me.

It turned out my friend hadn't had an allowance at all.

Her mother's pale face flushed.

I said I was sorry: I hadn't known her money was for communion. This was accurate, since I'd never heard of communion.

I'd pay my friend back in a week, I promised. As soon as I got my next allowance.

But no, said her mother bitterly. The damage had already been done.

Closing my eyes briefly, I resolved to give up my prize.

Anxiously I dug around in my paper bag and held out the gum in its yellow packet. Suggested *it* could be for communion.

The mother's frown deepened.

For the Lord and my father, who otherwise had a relationship of mutual disinterest, were in complete agreement when it came to the repulsiveness of chewing gum.

She snatched the yellow packet from my shaking hand. It would not be for the Lord, no sir. But neither would it be for me.

She ordered me to leave. I should think twice, her fury strongly implied, before I crossed her threshold again.

I'd stolen the dime from God—it had belonged to God himself.

I sniveled in self-pity as I embarked on the six-block walk back to my house.

Self-pity, I'd discovered, was luxurious—warm and soothing. When it became available to me, I liked to wallow in it.

I was a lowly thief.

And had no gum, either.

To bolster my spirits as I walked, I made up a morning song of my own. Sang it as I strode forward, faster and faster, then broke into a run. Away from the site of my humiliation—away, away, away!

Rise, and shine, and give God your gum gum gum gum, dime thief, of the, Lord.

FOR A WHILE, when my life was getting started, I believed the stories about winning—that effort and achievement would translate to success, with a little good luck thrown in. That life is a straight line, tending upward, and the market a meritocracy.

So when I met with personal failures, in school or in love or later in career, it was just evidence that I wasn't measuring up. Yet.

"Everything happens for a reason"—a saying at which, in the intervening years, I've come to recoil—was internalized. It kicked in as a reflex after a disappointment. Failure was karmic balance. Or a well-deserved judgment, meted out for a lack of talent or skill. A weakness of character.

All my failures were strictly my own, is what I believed with the naïveté of obedience. Like all my successes.

To look for answers to adverse events in systems or power structures, instead of individuals, was to weasel out of responsibility like a coward. To try to shift the blame onto a blameless machine.

PERSONAL FAILURES OCCUR, of course. Everyone has to fail sometimes. Strategically, the most successful cultural lies are those that find their foothold in such predictable occurrences, along with individual guilt complexes, fears, and petty insecurities.

The infamous "Crying Indian" ad campaign of 1970 is a case in point: in this one-minute spot an American actor of Italian descent named Iron Eyes Cody, dressed up as a Native American paddling a canoe and wearing a feather in his headband, wept silently as he beheld the litter with which careless individuals were despoiling his ancestral home.

Consumers should take on the task of cleaning up single-use plastic, was the ad's message. The problem was *them*. What the problem was *not* was the companies that made the plastic. And that were profiting handily from producing as much of it as they could sell, without regard for its disposal. Which, if they agreed to be accountable for it, would reduce their profit margins.

The core romance of capital depends on this deflection of guilt by promising wealth and freedom to the hardworking and worthy. Then shrugging off all failures to attain that wealth or freedom as simple verdicts of personal unworthiness.

It's not me, it's you, says capital.

Oh right—billions of you. Still. Totally not my fault.

FOR THOSE WITH vested interests, like corporations and politicians, as well as those in the knowledge industry like scientists and economists, there's always been pressure not to alarm the public, which votes and buys and behaves according to the information it receives from them.

To frighten the public is to run the risk of instability and even chaos—a threat to power structures, for sure, but also a threat to general welfare, when it comes to the climate. Since powerful governments, regardless of their merit, are crucial to making and enacting the laws and policies that can draw us down quickly from carbon.

So the public has to be gentled, like an unruly horse on the bit. For elected officials, sometimes, this means quashing high-stakes information and spreading reassurance on the narrative: Democracy is up to this task, and so is capitalism.

For the fossil fuel complex, it also means shifting responsibility onto other parties—often individual people.

During a crucial period for tackling the climate crisis, fossil companies knew the science and made a conscious decision to actively discredit it through expensive ad campaigns. They used language, of course: mollifying and tranquilizing words, pictures of green hills and blue skies. It was British Petroleum, not the environmental lobby, that promoted and popularized the term *carbon footprint*. To help convince people that their personal behavior needed to be modified and that would solve the problem.

They did this for half a century. At which point they were forced to cop to it.

But the companies brazened it out. They kept drilling and mining at a breakneck pace, with the full complicity of even moderate and purportedly climate-friendly administrations such as President Joe Biden's. They kept greenwashing fossil fuel use and strongly resisting a rapid conversion to clean energy, horrified by the prospect that their oil and gas leases, reserves, and massive property infrastructure might lose their value and turn into "stranded assets." The viability of fossils seems to exist, for them, in a void of other being, where nothing matters beyond private profit.

Clearly the duty of large-scale reform lies with capital and its instruments. Yet individuals will also have to be willing to adapt. In the short term, switch from gas-guzzling cars to electric ones and public transit; curb our appetites for clothing and trinkets and petrochemical products like plastic; change what we eat and drink. The citizens of rich nations consume animal flesh with gusto, though livestock are a leading cause of emissions and drive mass extinction through the large-scale conversion of ecosystems and landscapes.

To motivate change, some argue for hope over fear. Climate doomsaying, like the invocation of personal responsibility as a substitute for structural transformation, can feel like a psy-ops of despair. Encouraging apathy.

In fact hope and fear run alongside each other, indivisible. And fear and despair are not equivalent.

WHEN WE ACT at the last minute—or even, by some measures, after the last minute—we act in a panic, flailing and striking out at innocent bystanders. So the risk increases that a terrified focus on reining in climate change through desperate measures will ignore the urgent need to preserve, at the same time, the diversity of nature. Run roughshod over the rest of the physical world and the life-support systems it sustains.

The sped-up siting of mines for the production of lithium and other electric vehicle components, for example, in the habitat of endangered species who live nowhere else on the planet. The rapid buildout of solar and wind installations in the same. The swift plunder of the deep seabed for rare-earth minerals.

ENDLING ISN'T THE only new word in the emotional and ontological lexicon of extinction.

The term solastalgia was coined by an Australian philosopher, Glenn Albrecht, in 2004 to describe the complex feeling of longing and distress caused by wide-scale environmental destruction. I prefer the related terms species aloneness and species loneliness, which refer to the specter of a dawning era in which the solitude we already know—as individuals of a

deeply social species who are more and more shut off from our own physical communities—will be echoed by a greater silence gathering around.

Other new words, compiled and presented online by an artistic entity
that calls itself the Bureau of Linguistical Reality, include *shadowtime*,
referring to the feeling of living in two temporalities simultaneously—
the grandiose sweep of evolutionary time and the day-to-day time of
people. The concept of *shadowtime* denotes an awareness that the near
future is going to be drastically different from the present.

And then there's *epoquetude*, the bittersweet comfort of a realization
that, though the human species may not endure, some version of the natural world will live on after we're gone.

3

—

INSIDE A BOX of worn, once-beloved objects I keep a blue-and-gray plaid camel that used to be my father's. His mother had sewn it for him, and he'd carried it with him, as a child, across four continents.

When he was small, in the 1930s, his father was a diplomat, first a language officer and then a US consul in China. As a "China hand" his father had a household staffed and run as befitted members of the Mandarin scholar-gentleman class, reserved for the learned and for bureaucrats. They moved from Shanghai to Harbin, Chongqing, and Tientsin. In these cities my father was raised by a Chinese nanny, an *amah*, while his parents, Bus and Billie, were busy with their diplomatic functions.

With the *amah* my father spoke only Mandarin, which I'm told was his first language. Until he reached the age of five, she chewed his food before feeding it to him. Much like a mother bird.

This was a normal child-rearing practice, we were told, in the scholar-gentleman class, which would soon decline after the end of the Qing dynasty.

Presently this nanny, Nai Nai, was found to have tuberculosis and released from service. (Despite her feeding methods, my father never contracted the disease.)

I do not know what happened to Nai Nai after that.

In one of the earliest pictures I have of my father as a little boy he sits, wearing a hat and a neat jacket, atop a donkey outside one of his family's rental homes in China.

His parents are absent from the photo, as they are from most photos of his early life. Instead a male servant stands beside the donkey. And the boy.

CAMELS HAVE BEEN domesticated for thousands of years but seem to resent their servitude more than horses or donkeys. My mother tells of camel trains she saw in the Sahara Desert on excavation trips with my father—how every morning the animals, biting and spitting up their partially digested food, resisted their handlers in a spirited fashion.

A few wild Bactrian camels remain—the species is critically endangered. But the great majority have been exposed to radiation from Chinese bomb explosions at Lop Nur, the largest nuclear test site in the world.

Even irradiated, those camels persist.

ONE LETTER WRITTEN by my grandfather Bus to my grandmother Billie, whom I never knew, describes a luncheon he attended in Hanoi.

He'd been sent there to round up American missionaries and nuns. This was late August of 1945. Two weeks prior, the atomic bombs, so cutely named Fat Man and Little Boy, had been dropped on the people of Japan. Bus's assignment, my family believes, was to let the proselytizers know they should leave the area with all due haste: the US government wouldn't be able to protect them anymore. There'd been a coup in the region, and the new Marxist-Leninist regime wouldn't be so tolerant of Christian zealots.

He spoke to Trappist nuns through barred windows and to a Carmelite sister, who'd lived in devout seclusion for many years, through a metal screen with pinholes stamped in it. Recommending they return to the United States. For their safety.

But they were resistant to his entreaties, and—as with Nai Nai—we never learned their fates.

The luncheon he described was intimate by diplomatic standards. The Americans included him, a Colonel Nordlinger, and three officers. Their guests of honor were two local men, one named Ho Chi Minh, the other Bao Dai.

Ho Chi Minh was the Marxist leader of what would subsequently be called North Vietnam. A Soviet- and Chinese-allied intellectual, he would defeat the French empire at the Battle of Dien Bien Phu and, as a leader of the Viet Cong, also drive the defeat of South Vietnam and the United States in the Vietnam War. Eventually Saigon would be renamed Ho Chi Minh City.

Bao Dai was the newly deposed emperor of that country, previously called Annam. He was a puppet, first of the French, then of Ho Chi Minh's provisional government. Soon he would grow fully irrelevant to the workings of power and take himself off to France, where his status as a fallen monarch became a social calling card. He liked to dock his luxury yacht in Monaco.

Bao Dai was a partyer: a playboy, a gambler, and a collector of animal trophies.

Together the men enjoyed a nice lunch.

HO IS A SEASONED old professional revolutionary, reads my grandfather's letter.

The term *professional revolutionary* was what first caught my eye, as I went through the worn accordion file of his letters. It had never occurred to me that "revolutionary" could be a profession.

Bus's penciled script on the soft yellow foolscap—he was away from his typewriter—is still sharp, as if freshly scrawled.

As if, though he's been dead now for a quarter-century, he sat down to write it just a few minutes ago.

[Having] done time in French, Chinese, and even in Hongkong jails, [Ho Chi Minh] is amazingly pleasant . . . was years with the

Chinese Communists and came back here to head the Government in late August after the palace coup that eased Bao Dai out . . . The Emperor is very sophisticated (about 40 or 43) and apparently got a first-grade French education. He looks much like what you'd expect of a modern-day Rajah, and is said to be interested mainly in sports, chiefly hunting.

There is wonderful shooting a couple of hundred miles from here.

MY GRANDFATHER DIDN'T hunt, that I know of. But it has been suggested that Bao Dai—over the course of many hunts, fed, clothed, and fitted out in finery, with a retinue of faithful retainers—may have been almost single-handedly responsible for the extermination of Vietnam's wild tigers.

BUT THE BUSINESS of consorting with potentates didn't last long for Bus. During the Second Sino-Japanese War, he was interned by the Japanese Imperial Army for a year, separated from his wife and his children. Not long after he returned, Billie died of cancer and he was grief-stricken. Still, with three young children to take care of, he soon remarried.

My mother tells me Billie may have selected her successor for him when she realized her illness was terminal. She was anxious about her children's care.

What about that nice woman we met on the steps of the embassy? she's rumored to have asked him.

That woman, Helen, became his second wife.

I would later know her as my grandmother, or step-grandmother, technically, and though I was fond of her—I exchanged long letters with her for years, as I did with my maternal grandmother—*nice* isn't the word I would choose. *Rigorous,* maybe. *Intelligent. Proud* or *austere.*

The new couple had postings in Chile, Newfoundland, and Australia.

When Bus was let go from the diplomatic corps, he and Helen settled in a town outside Boston, in an area that had been his family's seat since the landing of their ancestors at Plymouth. They had two more children and a house in West Bridgewater, near Brockton, Massachusetts, in which one of my cousins and his family still live today.

That was the early 1950s, at the height of the McCarthy era, and many in the State Department felt the weight of McCarthyism.

Grampits, as we called him, had voted for a socialist presidential candidate in the 1930s—true. My father would describe himself as a socialist too, though as far as I know this was more of an abstract preference than a politics. I never saw him take direct action to elevate the fortunes of the proletariat.

So there was the force of the McCarthyites. But admittedly, in my grandfather's case, there was also the fact that the State Department had been left, after WWII, with a surplus of China hands.

Whatever the reason, Bus was honorably discharged. And afterward, in his depressed New England town, the diplomat who'd once shared a table with emperors and revolutionaries was unemployed for a long time. Helen, whom we called Tai Tai—*lady* or *married woman* in Mandarin— helped support the family by teaching. My grandfather took a temporary job as a night watchman, then another in a cabinet-assembly shop. In the end he secured a permanent position as a technical editor for a lighting manufacturer, housed in a nondescript suburban building, where he passed twenty years before retiring.

I LEARNED NONE of this from my father, but rather from my mother and my half-uncle Jack—his younger half-brother—long after both my grandfather and father were gone. And Tai Tai, too.

In the limited scope of my personal observation, as a child, my father was always distant from his own father in both space and emotion. They were polite, when they met on our rare, brief visits, but as distant to each other as two cold stars. In their politeness and wariness they seemed like shadows of a similar form—two shades that exist, in my memory, mostly in armchairs, gazing down at books.

Each with a quiet wit, for sure, but each also residing in the gray penumbra of an unnamed disappointment or division I would never understand.

IN CHRISTIANITY AND ISLAM, which together are professed by more than half of the world's people, the verbal profession of faith is necessary for belonging. Testimonies to the power of Jesus, and in Islam the recitation of the Shahada, are central pillars of the practice of belief.

Wordless beings, of course, are unable to profess a faith. So in these dominant forms of monotheism the beasts, who either have no language or do not share our own, have relinquished their right to a chance at eternal life.

In many cases—because of the privileges we extend to the speaking but deny to the unspeaking—to any life at all.

MY DAUGHTER WAS three months old when my father lay dying. My brother and sister and I took turns lifting her over his rented hospital cot, set up against a wall in the dimly lit dressing room next to my parents' bedroom.

We didn't know how much he could hear or comprehend, if anything. By then the cancer had spread to his brain.

He was sixty-nine and had never admitted to the reality of his death. So I didn't know what to say to him, because all that came to me was, repeatedly: You're dying.

But I was afraid any acknowledgment of the fact would frighten him. Even, somehow, hurt his feelings.

The unsaid stretched between us.

My father lived outside the self-disclosure culture so familiar to his children—confession was of no interest to him. He'd always used his dry, self-deprecating wit to deflect us when we approached the subject of the personal. Though he was kind and affable, he always seemed to find the expression of raw emotion distasteful.

Even now I'm jarred awake from time to time by a nightmare about the loneliness he may have felt in his final moments. He was rarely left by himself, in the dim room of his dying, but was cut off from the rest of us anyway. Isolate in the fact of his imminent departure. And unable to speak a single word.

In his last weeks, my mother told me—before she called us all to fly across the continent to his bedside—he'd tried to speak, at times. He'd been an eloquent man who held strong, immutable views on correct speech and pronunciation. As children we were forbidden, on pain of a sharp scolding, to aspirate the *h* in "forehead." And if one of us accidentally gave voice to a grammatical monstrosity like "She handed those plates to you and I," we'd be subjected to a tongue-lashing we wouldn't soon forget.

In his last weeks all that came out was gibberish. A word salad, my mother said.

He had lost the power of language.

I imagine the pathos of his isolation and try to make myself believe a different account: that in the half-light of his fading mind, the cliché about dying, that your life flashes before your eyes, came true. Except that rather than flashing, I like to think his life floated past him like a river, glittering in the sun. My father wasn't a man who relished speed: he never ran, he liked to say, except to catch a bus.

I like to think serenity enfolded him, in that fog of morphine, with old scenes drifting through the haze. Soft memories, say, from the time when we were babies, and he lay on his back on the floor, held our hands in his own, and flew us over him with our small, taut bellies balanced on the soles of his feet.

Or from the far-off reaches of his own boyhood, scenes I couldn't know but could only fabricate—a wooden trolley, maybe, creaking along its tracks in the amber light of a city afternoon. The large bats called flying foxes who dove and swooped in a park near his home in Melbourne.

A glimpse of snowy peaks over the skyline of another home he'd had, in Santiago, Chile.

Or the kind face of his younger sister Lucia, who had died young, of breast cancer like their mother, more than a dozen years before.

Her death, my mother has said since, left him alone as no other death had done.

IN DECEMBER AND January of 2020, at the height of the hottest and driest summer then on record for Melbourne, thousands of bats in the city's Yarra Bend Park died from the extreme heat—forty-five hundred in one three-day period alone. These were flying foxes, the largest bats in the world.

Similar die-offs occurred in Adelaide and Sydney. Fire trucks cruised slowly through the parks spraying water on the trees to try to cool the bats down; volunteer bat rescuers worked tirelessly to hydrate them using baby bottles and syringes.

Still, great piles of their bodies accumulated at the base of trees and had to be carted off in wheelbarrows.

THE DAY MY father died, sitting at his bedside, I held his hand and whispered—quickly and softly, as though to escape detection—*We all love you very much.*

Sometimes, recalling that scene, I feel a quick needle of alarm, afraid I may have said, *We all* loved *you very much.*

I hope not. I doubt it. But I'll never be sure.

Then, half embarrassed, I released his hand.

4

—

IT SEEMS ODDLY PERVERSE the way we insist, in movies and books, on making ghosts into monsters.

For ghosts are an aspiration to the afterlife: spirits with no need of a body. Personalities that live on, through a magical or supernatural transformation, liberated from death.

Ghosts, in the form of characters, are the realized hope that a soul can be set free.

But instead of being hopeful, our ghost stories are mostly horror shows. With a few exceptions in popular culture—such as the wildly successful and cringe-inducing movie *Ghost* from 1990—ghosts are threatening entities. They return to strike terror into us, to punish us, to upend lived reality.

As a culture we insist on seeing the spirits of the dead as revenge-seeking. Maybe this helps to alleviate a buried guilt, since we've become a people who rarely make an effort to remember those from whom we came—who no longer honor our ancestors.

Maybe we carry some guilt over this. As we deny the inevitability of our own deaths, we also deny the dead, releasing ourselves from the duty of memory.

And yet, we have to assume, none of the ancestors wished to be forgotten. As none of us wish to.

So we conjure up evil ghosts suspecting we deserve their anger.

In ghost stories we make the dead into murderers instead of givers of life. When in fact they were the mothers and fathers, stretching back over centuries, who brought us into being.

With that reversal of the real, the dead are turned into destroyers instead of creators.

And the erasure of the ancestors is vindicated.

FOR ME REGRET is the true ghost. Regret at having shown too little love.

WHAT IF THE trees went away? I heard one kid ask another.

The trees wouldn't *all* go away.

But what if they did?

The conversation ended.

IN FORGETTING THE PAST we forget everything. Our dismissal of the ancestors is also the dismissal of a far more expansive history—the history of what sustained them. Of forests and algae and oxygen, of fruits and flowers, rivers and seas. In forgetting the people who came before us we assume the aspect of self-made subjects, born out of only ourselves into each new day as it dawns. Us now and forever, or in the forever that is now. Now is the beginning that goes on and on, repeating.

This is the shifting baseline of expectation, where loss becomes invisible. A thousand trees, with their birds and their small burrowing mammals and foxes and clean, fragrant air, become a hundred.

Then twenty, then five.

Then none.

Once there were five trees here, we say. When I was young.

MY DAUGHTER AND SON have a near-zero interest in their bygone relatives. With the exception, in my daughter's case, of the ones who were witches. On my father's side of the family, back in the seventeenth century, there were some accused of witchcraft and others who did the accusing. When I told her this, her interest was briefly piqued.

But in their disengagement they're not alone: I knew nothing about my ancestors at their age. Or for decades afterward. My family lived in a country where it had no history—like many people displaced for varying reasons across wide spaces and national borders—so we only ever saw a trace of them in gravestones, when there was a family funeral to attend across the US-Canada border.

After my mother got engaged to my father, she went to meet his family. She was taken by my grandfather, on the very first day, to a cemetery in East Bridgewater, Massachusetts, where many Millets were buried. And proudly shown the plot reserved for her.

A chilly New England welcome.

For my grandfather's people death remained a stark reality. That could not be denied.

Since time, for us, is an arrow pointing to the right—like the Amazon logo—the past is barely real, a faded litany of names and dates whose details recede as we age. With the past turning irrelevant, no longer relived and remembered in material and ritual, everything tilts toward the present.

The future can't be seen or touched either, perpetually collapsing into the now, and is more and more abstract the further away it hovers. Unconsciously or semiconsciously we move along two tracks: our own individual futures, based on an imagined stability, and that of the world that will contain and decide them.

Our personal future is one we dare to conceive of—we must, we need to plan, we make our preparations, we try to set our young on a worthwhile path.

But the global future we unconceive. We stall when we think of it—stall, deny, bargain, or beg.

The life of the land, water, and atmosphere seems nebulous until we're struck, ourselves, by an episode of extreme weather. Or a geological event, which may or may not have been caused by fracking or human activities that drive subsidence or erosion. Even a pandemic, which may or may not have been caused by the trade in other animals and the plunder and liquidation of the forests they live in.

As long as the local seems normal, abnormalities that occur outside it stay hypothetical and chaos remains the province of others.

Meanwhile, in the vastness beyond our apartments and houses and neighborhoods, on a scale beyond our line of sight, creatures and green forms live and die. And their intricate and fragile harmony, evolved along with us over the eons, is upended.

The individual and global scales are interdependent, but to my generation, for a long time, the ligature between them seemed invisible.

Now the planning of personal futures, even among young persons of the comfortable middle class, is always tinged with second-guessing.

My daughter, like my son and most of their friends, is well aware of the looming chaos of climate change and species extinction. But still, when called upon to project herself into the future, she's always seemed to picture a progression of events neatly decoupled from the disintegration of norms.

Why not? What good does it do to plan for anarchy?

She would have a home in the Hamptons, she boasted to me when she was twelve or so. After she was all grown up. She would be a glamorous person. Hell, she already was.

She'd been there once or twice to visit friends. She'd wandered in and out of tony boutiques. And splashed in the ocean in a new bikini.

That swimsuit was named for an atoll in the Pacific where the US government tested nuclear bombs, I told her. It was marketed, when it came out, as atomic chic.

Pedantic, sure, but I was hoping it would make for good trivia.

Some of the islands are still more radioactive than Chernobyl or Fukushima, I added. *Now.* More than sixty years later.

Uh-huh, she said. Mama, I like it here. It's so pretty.

Elevation of East Hampton, I googled. Thinking of the time frame of her ambitions.

Sea-level rise, Long Island. Water table. Saltwater intrusion. Frequency of hundred-year floods.

THE WORD SPECIES was directly taken from Latin, where it was paired with *specere* ("to look") and used to translate the ancient Greek term εἶδος, meaning "a look," "a shape," or "a visible form." Plato raised the common term to high philosophy as the eternal, transcendent form of all things. But Aristotle, the West's first biologist and namer of five hundred animal species, brought it down to earth. Strongly but not exclusively associated with plants and animals after him, it came to primarily refer to such beings in common usage about four centuries ago.

The expanded version of Linnaean taxonomy that we use today—a system of eight categories that biologists and botanists use to organize the living, up from Linnaeus's three—is hierarchical. Debates occur about the system's validity, but it remains our standard for the biological classification of organisms. From top to bottom—from the general to the specific—the taxa go: domain, kingdom, phylum, class, order, family, genus, species. Under "species" we also sometimes define subspecies and populations.

By promoting a hierarchy of the natural world, some have argued, it also promotes a hierarchical model of human social organization. And possibly of human merit. In which some of us are "naturally" at the bottom, and others "naturally" at the top.

We live in the dry order of taxonomy but also in the afterglow of the once-revolutionary vision of the Prussian explorer and scientist Alexander von Humboldt, who—as Andrea Wulf wrote in *The Invention of Nature*—approached the natural world as an interconnected and interdependent system, replete with marvels of being.

Humboldt, who authored much-read books about his global travels along with encyclopedic natural history tomes like the multivolume *Cosmos*, was already predicting in the late 1700s—before the widespread

Western use of petroleum as a fuel—that deforestation for agriculture and timber would warm the climate.

His work was passionately embraced by many of his American contemporaries, from Thomas Jefferson to Henry David Thoreau and John Muir and scientists like Charles Darwin and Ernst Haeckel. He was discussing evolutionary theory when Darwin was just a boy.

Though Humboldt was staunchly opposed to all slavery, including American, he loved the promise of the young democracy. He admired the Indigenous cultures he encountered in South America, along with their ways of knowing, and rejected the term *New World* on the basis that the lands and peoples it held were only new to Europeans like him.

His holistic and rhapsodic view of nature, informed by the poetic sensibilities of friends like Goethe and Schiller, fed into Western feeling and thought mostly through those it inspired.

Humboldt's life is scarcely known in English-speaking countries now, unlike Darwin's or even Linnaeus's, but his name is everywhere. There are towns and counties, bays, rivers, glaciers, and peaks named after him. There are at least twenty species—Humboldt orchids and lilies in California, Humboldt martens in the Pacific Northwest, Humboldt squirrel monkeys and bats in South America, dolphins and snails and toads and beetles and hummingbirds.

For much of his long life he was the most famous scholar on the planet.

SPECIES ARE OF particular interest because, within their category, they can mate and produce fertile offspring. And every individual species is genetically distinct from all others.

Also—though geneticists scoff at such amateur "morphological" assessments—they're identifiable to the layperson: most species, among those animals we can see with the naked eye, look different, though it's also true that "cryptic" species exist who are only distinguishable from each other through genetic analysis.

Still, the Latin root word, "to look," is apt. On an intuitive level, we choose to look at other creatures through the lens of species because we see ourselves that way: not primarily as mammals or primates, our class and order, but as *Homo sapiens*.

We privilege our humanness over our other identities, defining ourselves by our differences from other animals rather than by our sameness. I've heard nursing mothers complain of feeling like cows, an obvious association since cows are the milk producers in our economy.

For me, when I was feeding my infants, it wasn't cows that came to mind. When I thought of cows I saw animals in stalls, their infants taken away and replaced by machines.

I was raised in a household where breastfeeding was not only the norm but an act of community service—my mother belonged to a support group for nursing mothers called La Leche League, which held regular meetings in our living room. I'd often wander in, as a small child, and see a dozen mothers breastfeeding their babies at once.

For me nursing was an earthier evocation—I felt more like a plump, furry wild creature in a burrow. Sheltered and sheltering.

Those were the days, now long past, when I knew myself most as a mammal.

When my toddlers and infants slept in my bed, and the dog slept there with us, I felt a contentment that was almost like completion.

We were a heap of mammals, warm and breathing. Together with our bodies, each dreaming a private dream.

THE TERM *ENDANGERED SPECIES* was adopted by US media in the 1960s and began to be used often around 1973, with the passage of a powerful law called the Endangered Species Act.

The act was passed almost unanimously—by a vote of 92–0 in the Senate and 390–12 in the House—and signed into law by a Republican president.

Personally Richard Nixon distrusted environmentalists, though he had a fondness for national parks and the tough, outdoorsman legacy of

Teddy Roosevelt. But Nixon presided over three Congresses with Democratic majorities in both houses, and those pushed hard for conservation and public-health statutes. In the early seventies, in the wake of Rachel Carson's book *Silent Spring*, public opinion favored environmental protection strongly—as it still does today.

So it was on Nixon's watch that most of the federal laws protecting the US environment—including the Endangered Species Act, the Clean Air Act, and the National Environmental Policy Act—were passed. Each of these laws is now used by public-interest groups to force an often unwilling government to safeguard our collective well-being.

MY KIDS GREW UP in the desert, in a sage-green landscape of tall cacti set against reddish mountains that rise dramatically out of gently sloping bajadas.

Our house, on the edge of a national park, is surrounded by wild animals. Diamondback rattlesnakes and tarantulas are common here, and in the yard we often see coyotes and mule deer and bobcats. Boar-like animals called javelinas, or collared peccaries—who have large heads and tiny, dainty feet—wander through the garden in herds. Hawks and owls alight on the thorny trees; cactus wrens and woodpeckers called flickers screech at us from saguaro cacti and prickly pears. Families of quail and lone roadrunners skitter across the sand.

Still my children, out in the rural Southwest, spend less time looking at animals than I did growing up in a big city. To them, for most of their late childhoods, the movement and colors of screens, full of human drama, were more compelling than animal bodies and habits.

The animals move slowly through time, by comparison to screen images. At an almost glacial pace.

Where's the plot? I can feel the children thinking as I point out animals to them. And they nod and move away.

Where's the dialogue? Where are the people?

But they know something I didn't.

Maybe it was living in a house without a TV and therefore having little exposure to nature shows like *Mutual of Omaha's Wild Kingdom* or David Attenborough's *Life on Earth*. Maybe it was my disinterest in the news, as a child—my parents had newspapers delivered, but I didn't read them; my mother listened to CBC, the Canadian Broadcasting Corporation, every day in the kitchen and in her car, but I tuned it out. Droning voices, signifying nothing.

Maybe it was simply my narrow field of view.

Whatever the causes, I didn't grow up with an awareness of the threat of mass extinction—I grew up knowing animals, but not knowing their peril. When I saw animals in my backyard or at the zoo, or looked at their pictures in books, my engagement with them wasn't accompanied by a looming story of loss.

It's different for my own children. For starters, they have two parents occupied in their daily jobs with the disappearance of the wild.

But they also inhabit, along with many in their demographic, a media world where the lives of free animals are rarely presented without a postscript to warn us of the tenuousness of these creatures' survival.

When the animals appear outside of logos and cartoonish renderings—when their lives are truly investigated on-screen—they come to us compromised by sadness. They have long shadows cast over their features, captured inside a darkening twilight of existence, always with a measure of guilt attendant to our glimpses of them.

The beasts are defined by their peril—even their suffering. As sacrificial victims in the history of human error.

5

LIKE ANY KIDS who spent a lot of time outdoors, my brother and sister and I became familiar with death, as well as life, through the others. Before we knew the death of a person, it was animal deaths, which happened all around us, that taught us about endings.

We saw dead insects: butterflies, whose wings disintegrated into powder when you touched them, and pill bugs, cold and curled into balls, in the rock garden. We saw dead birds: robin and sparrow chicks fallen from nests onto the sidewalk.

In grade school I picked up bugs and kept them in a transparent plastic box on my desk that I referred to as my Dead Pet Collection. I liked the morbid reverberations of the phrase—it reminded me of the illustrated books of Edward Gorey, which I admired—and hadn't heard of serial killers yet. So I didn't know it made me sound like one.

The box was no polished museum display case, but I did have standards: I never touched the houseflies whose dull gray-black bodies lay bundled in cobwebs in our metal window troughs.

Felt no impulse to gather in those humblest of the dead.

HIDDEN IN THE lilac bushes and weeds, I found beetles and moths and jewel-green cicadas. On tree trunks we saw the cicadas' brown, papery exoskeletons, empty but clinging to the bark.

I never killed an insect for my collection, only scavenged for their bodies. Fatalities did occur, though, as a result of our annual cocoon hunts. In spring we picked cocoons off branches and wooden fences and stuck them in jars, with a few leaves and twigs.

Some of the neighborhood parents condoned our cocoon-harvesting in the name of scientific education; others condemned it as wasteful and inhumane.

We punched holes in the lids and waited for the butterflies to emerge.

In fact they would have been moths—since butterflies make chrysalids out of the hardened bodies of their pupae, not cocoons spun from silk—but we didn't know the difference.

Most times, our waiting was in vain.

I REMEMBER SUMMERTIME by the high, whining song of cicadas, a metallic buzz so constant it turned into background noise. I remember fall by the piles of maple leaves along the street, red, yellow, and orange. We liked to play with the maple keys, which whirled like helicopters when you dropped them, and jumped and rolled in the crisp airiness of the piles.

I remember winter by the banks of snow so high you could burrow into them and make snow forts. And spring by the melting of that snow, its lacy crusts stretching along expanses of brown grass.

Some people I've met are able to unfurl their memories like calendars, with events pinned precisely to days, months, and years.

My own are more like a dream—the shifting landscape you might see from a train window, interrupted by monuments that appear out of the haze. With edges lit by longing or regret.

Here's a house somewhere in the country. Don't know where, don't know whose. I just know we swung on a tire that hung from an old, spreading tree.

The house had a wraparound porch, with handrails painted white. After the sun set, we saw fireflies blinking among the bushes, drifting over the grass.

Elsewhere, near the shore of Lake Ontario, I recall a jovial, portly man riding a tricycle the size of a car. We liked him very much and called him Uncle Tony, though he wasn't our uncle but my father's colleague and good friend.

Or I see a young man with long, dark hair, wearing a kilt, dancing and falling down at a party. Outside was a large, well-tended garden in which his mother grew roses. In Argentina in December, where it was summertime.

But my mother tells me the tricycle was only the size of a normal bike. The man at the party, my favorite college boyfriend, says that he never fell. He recalls bleeding from a surgical cut, then lying on a bed while his mother and I sopped up the blood from the incision.

Although his mother died some years ago—in a car accident along with his father—he still knows the names of her favorite roses.

Albertine, Penelope, Sally Holmes.

FIREFLIES, A FAMILY made up of around two thousand species, are airborne beetles that fly by night and flash their luminescence. Different species flash in different patterns; some flash in unison.

They always looked magical to us, floating like fairy lights in the gloaming. But they're less common now than they were when I was young. Researchers aren't sure why, but most suggest it's the obvious: the development and paving over of their marshes and forests. And possibly the confusion and disorientation caused by light pollution.

In 2022, in a tiger reserve in India where pristine forest remains, filmmaker Sriram Murali captured a video of billions of synchronous fireflies turning the dark into a dancing light show of yellow and green.

WE HAD FAR FEWER TOYS, my siblings and I, than my children have had. But we played with those few toys far more often. As we played more with the artifacts of nature—inspecting them, collecting them, and sometimes destroying them.

With the neighborhood kids we made disgusting potions out of found substances, from leaves to feces and bird skulls and insects. We costumed ourselves in our parents' discarded clothing, available to us in a "dress-up" box, and traipsed along the block carrying toy weapons and sticks. Poking at bushes and each other. We played hide-and-seek through other people's property and spread scary witch rumors about a lonely old lady who lived down the street. Performed backyard singing concerts featuring *The Sound of Music* with sprigs of lilac stuck into our hairbands.

Once, in Georgia for the summer, we tried our hand at perfume-making. We picked magnolias and crushed their petals into a mush, then stuck the mush into mason jars full of tap water. "Infusing" the water with their scent and straining out the larger pieces.

When we decided the mixture was ready, we'd glue labels on the jars and go up and down the block selling the jars door to door.

We got rid of quite a few.

Because our perfume *did* smell good. For a day or two.

After that it smelled rotten.

MAGNOLIAS MAY HAVE BEEN the first flowers on earth: they date back to the Cretaceous, starting 145 million years ago. Likely they pre-existed bees—who are believed to go back 130 million years but whose oldest fossils date back a mere 80 million—and are pollinated instead by beetles.

IN ELEMENTARY SCHOOL I had a classmate who liked to pick earth-worms out of puddles after a rain. She was the opposite of a germaphobe:

a germaphile, maybe. She also picked up wads of used bubble gum—not hers—from the underside of desks or from the sidewalk. When they seemed fresh enough, I guess. Lickety-split, she'd pop them into her mouth.

At the time I was repulsed. Naturally.

Now I remember her for this uncommon boldness. Which, as far as I knew, never once made her sick.

She was tough.

I called the earthworms slimy and shuddered at the sight. Once, when a boy dropped one in my hair, I screamed and started a fight. I kicked his chair out from under him; he chased me as I walked home and punched me in the stomach. So hard that I collapsed.

My classmate picked up the earthworms, while I ran from them.

But those lowly worms were hiding their light.

Did I bother to learn they're hermaphrodites? I did not.

Did I know that many species reproduce without a partner, in a virgin birth?

Also no.

AS THEY GREW OLDER, my children played outside less and less—outdoor pastimes occupied a smaller and smaller fraction of their waking hours. For both of them, as for the rest of us, the power of living nature was diminishing before the captivation of the screens.

And yet for Sy, as a teenager, it was time in the wild that lifted him up. On a wilderness program in the Tonto National Forest, when he was fifteen, he learned to make fire with a bow drill he'd built and to locate water and forage for some of his food. He fashioned a spear by carving found jasper into a spearhead, and with it caught numerous fish. He was taught to follow the paths of animals. He learned myths from the Lakota cosmology and the wisdom of an elder named Ezekiel.

"We ate lilies," he wrote me in a letter, "that tasted like potatoes."

In the forest and the desert his small band of children slept under the sky without tents. For nine weeks he never entered a building and never looked at a phone.

Every night the band made a fire and sat around it, and most mornings they rose and walked for several miles.

ONE CHRISTMAS, WHEN I was little, I was given a five-year diary with a red leather cover and gold-edged pages. You were supposed to record your doings and feelings, then lock it up with a miniature key so that no one else could discover them.

It was a handsome notebook. The pages were smooth and crisp. For several weeks I wrote in it every day. Shameful secrets, furtive private pleasures. Sharp observations of my siblings, who, since they were younger, irritated me.

Then I lost interest. What was the point of writing down your feelings if no one else would ever read them?

I left the journal unlocked for a while, hoping to cause a scandal. But no one bit.

It was a confession without an audience.

Outside the diary, I went from eight years old to thirteen. Inside the diary, the pages stayed blank.

Four years and eleven months passed without incident.

And I've never kept a journal since.

LIKE THE VELVETEEN RABBIT in a well-known picture book, our toys desperately wanted to be real. We bestowed this desire on them—it was only natural. As our playmates they wished to be allowed to *feel*. The way we did.

Also, they wished for agency. The way we did. To be allowed to *do*.

The pretty dolls we dressed up in pretty clothes, or, in our more rageful moods, impulsively ripped a leg off. The soft teddy bears arranged around our beds to look like an audience—one that fully appreciated our chosen activities, no matter how tedious and repetitive they were. The soldiers that stood on plastic puddles with their rifles raised, the match-box cars that could go anywhere as we made *vroom vroom vroom* noises.

The toys were ensouled, when we were little. Like the animals.

But over time they lost the souls we'd given them and turned into mere objects.

MY BABY BROTHER'S favorite animal was the cheetah—the fastest land mammal, he liked to tell anyone who would listen. "It can go from zero to sixty in only three seconds," he used to say.

He was little enough to be proud of this ability. By proxy. Proud of those cheetahs, so far away in Africa, who didn't know how much he revered them.

Years later he would pronounce the very same words, *It can go from zero to sixty in only three seconds*, when I visited him in LA and he drove me around in his electric car.

At that moment his old attachment to cheetahs came rushing back to me—to cheetahs and to all the other animals he'd cataloged in the rambling, ambitious "Encyclopedia of Animals" he'd exhaustively researched, written, and illustrated as a child.

He'd been a boy with a bestiary.

These days fast driving is less alluring to Josh than to plenty of other drivers—with two children in the back of his vehicle, he typically proceeds at a reasonable pace—but as he extolled the virtues of the car, I saw the same admiration on his face I'd seen some forty years before. As he extolled the virtues of cheetahs.

IN THE YEARS before my parents bought a TV, when I was twelve—forced to buy it, more or less, by embarrassment as their children constantly loitered around the houses of neighbors and friends who owned one—we had spent our weekend afternoons reading. Alone in our bedrooms or all together, assuming loose, relaxed positions on the chairs and couch in the living room.

The cats would curl up beside us. Everything quiet except for the flick of pages as they turned.

Remembering those afternoons makes my childhood feel quaint. Because even for dedicated readers like my family—even for me, who ended up making a living as a writer—the book's power was already shrinking with dazzling speed.

It was a change of material, in part, since books are made from softwoods like spruce, pine, and fir. Treated with preservatives, they're the embalmed, processed bodies of trees, overlaid with words. Timber, after all, was the mainstay of extractive economies before the dominance of coal and oil.

For quite a while our stories, like our factories, depended on it.

With the shift to film and video, our stories began to be told on media of polymer and metal alloys, enabled by computers that were also made of by-products of the oil and gas industry.

The new stories relied on fossil fuels for their production and delivery.

We barely noticed that; what we noticed, when we noticed anything, was the momentum of the new stories. Where books were a dialogue between writer and reader and lay motionless until our hands touched them, our eyes saw them, and our minds interpreted them, the movies and shows did not demand our deliberate and solitary attention. Instead they descended on us in a whirl of sight and sound, lifting us into elsewhere with their color and movement, their musical scores that told us how and when to feel.

The movies and shows didn't have one author but were created by, and designed for, many. Crowd fare. We could watch them alone or in a group—over time, when the technology allowed it, we would often return to a solitude of story consumption—but what enthralled us was their multisensory simulation of life.

Even, it has to be admitted, the grand luxury of passivity they invited:

there you would be, exercising no conscious judgment, decoding no private language, searching no internal dictionary.

Endlessly entertained.

Some of us still read books—enjoy the feel of them in our hands, value the intimate companionship and insights they offer. The speaking of one mind to another across the fields of time.

But do they capture us in their velocity? Sing and dance for us, show us the faces of angels, catch us up in waves of orchestrated feeling?

Do they speak to us out of the dark like oracles?

BACK IN THE 1990s, before high-quality digital content was available and when there wasn't much else on TV, a lot of us watched police procedurals. Popular shows like *Law & Order*, and after it *CSI*, had many spin-offs.

We liked to watch fictional authorities mete out justice to violent criminals, which made for thrilling drama. And helped to reassure us that such justice existed.

Crimes against individuals are fascinating to us—maybe partly because, as the English mystery writer P. D. James said, the solving of such interpersonal violations represents a restoration of the social order. And thus is, as James herself was, essentially conservative: the assignation of guilt and dispensing of justice to criminals amounts to a vindication of the status quo.

Meanwhile, the stories of crimes far greater in magnitude—against groups or classes—often remain untold.

In one show I saw, a violent offender decided to enter a guilty plea. He was such a handsome criminal it made you think, Wow, why'd *that* guy turn to crime? He could have been an actor!

Trying for a lighter sentence, he chose to do what his public defender called "allocute." This meant he'd make a statement to the court expressing his remorse. He'd tell the tale of his infraction. Explain why he'd committed it and show that he knew right from wrong. Perform an apology.

If you want a judge to be lenient, you have to use language. As in a confessional.

You have to say what you did.

OUR BRAINS' PLEASURE CENTERS respond to certain kinds of experience with rushes of neurotransmitters like serotonin and dopamine and endorphin, which excite and uplift us. Love, exercise, music, drugs, gaming and gambling, religiosity—all these and more give us highs.

The neuroscience of pleasure is only just emerging, but it's clear that in all these arenas novelty is a trigger: we're seduced by the delights of the new.

So we can easily be convinced to drop an old partner for a fresh model. More than half of us who take a lifelong vow to a husband or wife later recant those vows and get divorced, often simply because we meet someone newer. Romantic love and sexual desire—strongest in the first moments of relationships—function in our brains like substance addiction. The calm attachment of old bonds pales in comparison, and we're easily persuaded that resistance is futile.

But when the new love ages, our neurotransmitter injections and pleasure subside.

Pleasure addictions make it hard to know the difference between loving and wanting. With our possessions, as well as our personal bonds, desire and its satisfaction are the axes we spin on.

For those of us who—guided by wanting and getting—let the rest of the world slip away, the hour seems late to plead innocence.

But maybe not too late to allocute.

AS WE GROW older we call our toys by other names and resist the urge to imbue them with character or soul. Still, we remain vested in numerous objects that bring us satisfaction: we arrange and rearrange them, replace and improve them, gaze at them and sometimes play with them. We see an object and decide that we like it. And since we like it, we should own it.

Once we own it, we do show-and-tell. Some of us with subtlety. Others with naked pride.

The translation from seeing and liking to owning seems natural. Ownership is how we demonstrate appreciation and create a scene for display, advertising ourselves to each other, potential mates, allies, and sometimes competitors in the marketplace.

We're a nation of collectors who call the practice "hoarding" only when it's conducted in a dirty or ugly place. In TV shows like *Hoarders*, for example, the act of collecting is presented as clear evidence of mental illness—chiefly because the collections it features involve goods with little to no resale value.

Collection is sane and rational when it's done by those with economic privilege. But when it's conducted by those without wealth or prestige, in the cramped and unpleasant spaces such people command, we call it hoarding. And see it as pathology.

The hoarding middle- or upper-class people do is rarely a matter of need, though sometimes we make an argument for need in order to fulfill a desire. A newly minted food processor, say, seems better than the two we have already. The very existence of this superior form beckons to us.

So we say that we need it.

I've owned a string of toasters, for example, in an ascending order of attractiveness and unit cost. I now believe my current toaster to be the loveliest of all possible toasters. When I catch sight of other counter appliances made by the same Italian company, each similarly well-proportioned and colored in a semi-opaque, retro hue, I wish I could own several more.

Each in a manner of our choosing, we gather up bright baubles and place them in our nests.

Much like certain birds. Or the pack rats that live around my house and have succeeded, on several occasions, in invading it.

"PACK RAT" IS the common name for the desert wood rats that are abundant in the Southwest. They're sweet-looking animals with large, round ears and big eyes, but also the bane of my existence.

They build massive nests of dead cactus and twigs in welcoming, protected hollows and will also pull random-seeming objects into their middens. Ripped-up insulation and cloth that soften their bedding—this makes sense to us—but also plastic containers and other pieces of what looks like garbage.

Recently a pack rat who lives in the ground beneath my water heater, in a small, fenced yard set aside to protect our dog from coyotes, has begun to surround the two entrances to her nest with piles of dog shit we haven't cleaned up fast enough.

Maybe, with their strong odor, they serve, as the pieces of cactus do, as barriers against would-be intruders. Or maybe, once they're dragged farther into the nest and left to decay, they function as space heaters.

We remove the dog shit from the entryways with metal tongs. My boyfriend Aaron shakes his head as he does this, as though participating in an intervention for an addict. Tough love.

"It's for your own sake," he'll say to the rat. "You think you want these, but trust me, they don't make you look good."

If your house, like mine, lacks a garage, the pack rats can ruin your cars, whose engines provide a comforting warmth they enjoy nesting in. During their nest-building they gnaw away on wires. Then, all of a sudden as you're driving along, the car malfunctions. Multiple warning lights go on. If the rats have chewed through an important wire, this can be dangerous. Recently a rat gnawed through two lines leading to the two fuel tanks in both our cars on the very same night. Both fuel tanks had to be replaced, and the damage amounted to about three months' worth of my salary.

They invade living spaces with remarkable speed, chewing on the wires there too—lights and coolers and phones can stop working. One recently climbed into the house from the clothes-dryer vent to the outside. She stole an apple from a bowl on the kitchen table and chewed through my daughter's prom dress, hanging in a closet.

Because of pack rats, I gave up on landlines years before my urban friends did.

One time the rats built a nest in the crawl space between my roof and ceiling that was so large and heavy the ceiling began to sag. Workers came and tore out the Sheetrock; hundreds of pounds of dead cactus and rat corpses and droppings showered down into my front hall.

6

SEVERAL FEATURES OF animal bodies have evolved and disappeared, then re-evolved over the history of the planet. Eyes, for example, both simple like people's and compound like various arthropods', have come and gone and come again.

But species have not.

Species, as far as we know, don't come back.

They evolve or die off, but they don't recur.

They're singular creations of deep time.

A FEW GENETIC ENTREPRENEURS are working to reengineer extinct lifeforms and raise them from the dead, calling it "de-extinction." The media sometimes seizes on these technocratic enterprises as good-news stories.

Among such projects is one that involves finding the intact nucleus of a mammoth cell and out of it cloning a new mammoth.

It's unlikely that such clones could produce a viable population, even on a physical level, since the lack of genetic diversity in the originating samples would doom them to weakness and make them highly vulnerable to disease.

But even if the bodies of those long extinct could be remade from cells, their minds and behaviors, group dynamics, and feeding and reproductive strategies could not. Much as human beings' could not. Or those of Cro-Magnons or Neanderthals.

To try to re-create a human being from genetic material would be monstrous—a Frankenstein project. And yet, somehow, to try to do the same with other animals passes as laudable.

Attempts to rebuild complex animals from pieces of organic matter speak less to our technical expertise than to the lack, in parts of our scientific establishment, of extra-technical wisdom—a willful blindness to our hard-won historic graduation from the mechanistic reductions of Descartes. A rejection of the understanding that the other animals, like us, are not machines made out of flesh, but social and experiential constructs whose whole is much greater than their parts.

Each species is the delicate sum of an unrepeatable past.

That past, with its impossibly long series of events and landscapes and wide array of other animals and plants and fungi and bacteria, arranged in a complex and inscrutable interdependence, can never be duplicated.

And made us all who we are.

AMONG THE ENDLESS array of animals who have shaped human behavior are snakes, provoking a primal terror reaction even when they aren't venomous. The "abnormal" wariness of snakes is a common phobia—in some cultures, the single most common. We invest these reptiles with numerous evil qualities: it was a serpent, after all, who tempted us out of Eden.

And maybe there's some scientific validity to that, if the tree of knowledge is seen as a metaphor for the development of our minds.

A line of anthropological thinking called "snake detection theory," developed by a behavioral ecologist named Lynne Isbell in 2006, proposes that some primates' sharp vision—such as ours—evolved partly as a response to the presence of poisonous snakes. Primate species that evolved in places without those snakes don't tend to have such acute vision.

While some ground-based mammals evolved an immunity to snake venom, Isbell says, others, such as arboreal primates, developed sharp vision instead.

Neuroscientists are now working to find physical evidence to support her idea.

Which suggests that snakes, who were already around when the first mammals appeared but developed their venom-dispensing capabilities later, were key to building the capacity of the human brain.

Other scientists have suggested our sharp vision evolved so that we could pick out insects on branches.

Since we liked to eat insects, back when we lived in the trees.

ENVIRONMENTAL ECONOMISTS—ONE OF which, if you set store by graduate degrees, I'm supposed to be—call the gifts that other animals and plants give us, or which we take from them, their "use value." This is part of an arithmetic that aims to quantify the services of other beings to our kind in tools like cost-benefit analysis.

But the value of those services is limitless.

After the K-T asteroid impact, some 66 million years ago, a great planetary cooling occurred and—probably for one to two years—photosynthesis largely shut down. Three-quarters of plant and animal species suddenly died out, and widespread deforestation ensued.

Fungi exploded in number. Out of the decaying matter of the numberless dead, a massive fungal bloom emerged.

Some scientists have suggested that it was this explosion of fungi, along with the cold, that prevented a new evolution of large reptiles like dinosaurs and allowed for the rise of mammals instead.

Being cold-blooded, reptiles would have had a greater susceptibility to fungal pathogens. And fungi may have been more palatable to mammals than reptiles.

If those scientists are correct, it would mean the asteroid that hit Mexico was responsible for our existence.

So far, the internal temperature of our bodies—98.6 degrees Fahrenheit, on average—has largely kept fungi from invading them.

But fungi can adapt to warmer temperatures. One such, *Candida auris*, has been identified by the Centers for Disease Control as an emerging human-health threat.

Our debt to the other lifeforms, of course, stretches further back in time than that—even before there were vascular plants, even before there were trees, there were cyanobacteria, also called blue-green algae. Their appearance, some two billion years ago, produced the free oxygen that created a breathable atmosphere. This caused the first real mass extinction we know of, though it's usually not given a place in the canon of mass extinctions: it didn't kill off complex, multicellular life. The life around at the time was anaerobic—mostly bacteria in the ocean.

Bacteria were poisoned by the oxygen and died. But the Great Oxygenation Event allowed for the development of many new creatures.

Including us.

TO EXPLAIN WHY monkeys no longer live wild in Canada or the United States, an anthropologist named Noel Boaz refers to "the ascendancy of the rodents."

Boaz is interested, among other matters, in historical climate patterns as a force in human evolution. Near the end of the epoch called the Eocene, he's written, climatic cooling in the higher latitudes made fruit trees rarer, and nut trees, whose fruits have hard shells to protect them, more common.

With nuts, primates were at a disadvantage—we still have to crack them open with tools.

But rodents, with their constantly growing incisors, were in luck.

Squirrel-like rodents replaced the primates that once lived here some

45 million to 34 million years ago. According to Boaz's hypothesis, the squirrels took over those primates' niches in the trees.

Without the squirrels, he postulates, we might still have monkeys here.

IN THE WILD, most plants and trees travel only across the generations, as the seeds or pollen that produce their offspring are dispersed by birds or mammals or insects. Or water and wind. So they're deeply dependent on complexes of pollinators that are at increasing risk of extinction—including, according to the United Nations, about 40 percent of invertebrate pollinators worldwide.

Like Victorian children, the plants are seen but not heard: seen by us all around as they steadily capture the light and turn it into everything we need. Heard only when the breezes move their bodies.

Because they can't travel by themselves, we often view plants as passive and nearly inert. But, as with most kinds of otherness, what they lack in familiar attributes they offer in unfamiliar ones.

The greenness of plants is caused by conservative behavior—they look green to us because they reflect that wavelength of solar radiation. Yet most of the sun's energy comes from rays in the green part of the spectrum. Plants reject those rays in photosynthesis partly because they create "noise and inefficiency" in their systems.

Since they can't run away from predators, they've evolved to have no irreplaceable organs (unlike people, who can't lose their hearts or brains and keep going).

Many, notes plant scientist Stefano Mancuso, can have up to 90 percent of their "bodies" cut away without being killed.

ALONG WITH THE loss of their utility to us, extinctions mean that the gifts of a species' intelligence also vanish.

And of those possible gifts, we understand little.

Besides other species' "use value," the complex prism of their experience is lost. Their points of view and way of operating in the world are subtracted from the whole, along with the structure that supports them. Both hardware and software are erased.

One problem with this, leaving aside the sadness inherent in a life-form's end, is that since we didn't design the systems of biological existence, we have no reliable guide to their workings—no blueprints or manuals. So when we call in technicians to try to correct an imbalance we've created in nature, their interventions often go badly astray.

In thousands of cases where we've brought animals or plants with us when we colonized or traveled, both on purpose and by accident, we've caused the destruction of other species and natural systems—a process that has accelerated in recent years with our global mobility. Despite growing awareness of the pitfalls, there continue to be cases of deliberate introduction aimed at solving a problem that end up creating far more, in a cascade of imbalances and die-offs.

The history of this "importation biocontrol," where one non-native species is brought in to combat another, is rife with disasters.

Mosquitofish, imported to several countries to eat the mosquitoes that spread malaria, have multiplied dramatically in places where they don't belong. But mosquito larvae aren't their favorite food: they prefer fish larvae, so their presence drives native fish into scarcity.

In northern Australia, Florida, and numerous islands where sugar is grown, cane toads from the mainland neotropics were imported in the 1930s to eat the beetles that were damaging sugar crops. In Australia they proved fairly ineffective against the beetles, since they're not much for climbing and the beetles live at the tops of the plants. But the continent has no native toads, and the cane toads' sudden superabundance triggered a chain of species declines as the toads outcompeted native lizards, snakes, and crocodiles.

When the predator populations crashed, prey species multiplied. Bringing further cascades of damage to local plant communities.

In the United States, Hawaii has been a killing field for biocontrol projects as well as a hot spot of extinctions—these islands, which account for 0.29 percent of the country's landmass, are home to over 40 percent of the species now protected under the Endangered Species Act.

Introduced predaceous snails are driving the mass disappearance of native snails; mongooses brought in to get rid of rats—again for the sake of sugar crops—have wreaked havoc on endemic birds and have a voracious appetite for sea turtle eggs. They now run amok on all but two of Hawaii's islands, as well as on other islands of the tropics like Fiji and Jamaica.

But they didn't solve the rat problem, since, as it turned out, the mongooses are daytime workers. While the rats come out at night.

ABOUT ONE-THIRD OF biocontrol interventions have ended in the "establishment of a new natural enemy." Less than one-sixth have resulted in the successful control of the target pest.

The many factors we've omitted to consider in our biocontrol operations, which later rise up to dole out unwelcome surprises, are a red flag to those who advocate for ambitious "geoengineering" solutions to the climate problem.

These include a proposal to engage in the large-scale pumping of ozone-destroying sulfate aerosols into the atmosphere to cool it—a scenario various writers of science fiction have played out in recent novels. Also the dumping of iron dust into the oceans to trigger algal blooms and the genetic modification of crops to increase their carbon uptake.

There are also plans to block solar radiation by mechanical means that range from the deployment of huge, heavy sunshades to the placing of fifty-five thousand orbiting, wire-mesh mirrors, each forty square miles wide.

All of these schemes come with serious failure risks. When it comes to ambitious tinkering with the underpinnings of physical life support, our résumé—including its "Other Skills"—is made up of a list of breathtaking mistakes.

QUITE A FEW BIRDS, including European starlings, were brought to the so-called New World by design. A group called the American Acclimatization Society gave itself the mission—in retrospect, misguided—to bring over a favored list of species from the Old World. In order to uplift and improve the New.

There are now about 85 million starlings in North America, though not all are descended from the individuals the Society brought in.

Starling calls can be raucous, faithfully copying sounds ranging from other birds' calls to car alarms and the human voice. Their skills as mimics rival those of the Australian lyrebird, which looks like a fairy to me. It has a cross-seeming, sharp little face, but the rest of its form is like an ethereal dream, with plumage like downy white clouds bordered by two long, boldly striped arcs spread above it like wings.

To attract the attention of a mate, a male lyrebird finds an open patch on the forest floor. There he gives a concert while displaying, with sculptural shaking and fluttering movements, his lovely feathers.

His performance is an extended medley, consisting of perfect imitations of the songs and calls of dozens of other bird species that live in the forest around him. As well as other sounds he replicates faithfully, such as the click of a camera shutter and the whir of its small motor.

And even—almost as though the lyrebird has a grasp of irony—the chain saws of nearby loggers as they cut down trees.

WHEN ANIMALS PLAY DEAD, from possums to snakes to ducks, biologists don't usually suggest that they're doing so because they understand what *dead* is, as it pertains to themselves. Rather this death-feigning behavior—TI, or tonic immobility, which looks like paralysis—is mostly interpreted as a stress adaptation. Though people, too, can exhibit tonic immobility: for us the stress adaptation appears during extreme trauma, such as sexual assault. And war.

With the other animals, tonic immobility comes into play in self-defense, to avoid death by predation. It also manifests in mating, as when male sharks bite females and the females freeze. Occasionally it shows up in ways that look more like strategy than a response to stress.

Predatory East African fish called sleeper cichlids lie down on their sides on the bottom of Lake Malawi—the only place they live—then go perfectly still. And make their scales look blotchy. Possibly for camouflage, or to look as though they're decomposing.

When a scavenger fish draws near, attracted to the apparent corpse, they swiftly flick themselves upright. And eat it.

I can't help wondering if the show of blotchiness, like negative capability, is a mark of genius.

7

IN MY EARLY TWENTIES, before I went to grad school, I had a job copyediting a gun lovers' magazine called *SWAT: For the Prepared American.* One of the higher-ups at the magazine company believed that, as a copy editor responsible for correcting factual mistakes, I needed to know the magazine's subject matter better. And it was true that I barely understood the difference between a shotgun and a rifle.

He offered to take me to a shooting range.

It didn't occur to me to refuse his invitation, so I followed him in my car out of Beverly Hills, where we worked, to a gun club in a grimy area of Los Angeles where real estate was far less premium. He'd brought along some guns for us to use—including a dainty, small-caliber model since, he explained, I was female—and a stack of homemade paper targets.

Many club members seemed to have come in with their own targets. There were the basic kind that look like dartboards; stylized silhouettes of human heads-and-torsos you see in cop shows; a rearing bear and an eight-point buck. Nowadays there's a greater variety available for printout: I've seen an alien with an elongated head and suction-cup fingers, a fifties-style robot, a *Star Wars* stormtrooper, and a full-color Hillary Clinton.

But the higher-up's targets, which I only got a good look at after he clipped one onto the line and ratcheted it to the far wall for us to shoot at, were dot-matrix printouts of the faces of women and racial minorities.

Not exclusively—I think there were a couple of white men in the lineup too. Enough for cover. They were clearly thugs, unshaven and mean-looking.

I was so disoriented by the faces that a laughable number of my shots missed their mark. Afterward I wondered if he'd taken me to the club to show me his targets as much as his guns.

The second time I shot was decades later, with a painter friend named Dimitri who'd been in the Russian army as a younger man. He'd patrolled the area around Chernobyl after the core meltdown and brought his old service piece to my house.

I took it from him gingerly, half wishing I had a Geiger counter to test it with. We aimed at a piece of rotting plywood we'd set up in my backyard. My neighbors frequently shot off their guns in their own yards, to the north and east of me, and the target was only ten feet away. So I didn't give the legality of our shooting there a second thought.

Even at close range, though, my aim was poor. The gun felt wrong in my hand, with a weight beyond the physical. Its heaviness was magnetic—a dull, latent power I couldn't bring myself to trust.

It seemed to possess an invisible force field, as though, rather than me holding it, the gun was holding me.

A FIRST COUSIN of mine who lives in Georgia was congratulated by his soon-to-be wife on Facebook, in 2015, for the number of doves he'd taken down on a quick hunting trip to Córdoba, Argentina.

It must have been a canned hunt, where guides flush out birds for tourists to shoot, for the number was 5,006.

THE FIRST COUSINS I'm closest to, two brothers named Ben and Nick on my father's side, grew up in a converted barn on the edge of a cranberry bog outside the small town of Pembroke, Massachusetts. (Where they were friends, in their teens, with my now-boyfriend Aaron.) Ben and

Nick's parents were my father's sister Lucia, a librarian, and her husband
Richard, a talented artist who in his day job designed commercial logos
for the likes of supermarket chains, fruit drink companies, and banks.

My parents got along famously with Lucia and Richard, who'd worked
with my father on expeditions to Egypt before children were in the mix.

Visiting them one summer, at the tail end of the seventies when I was
still in grade school, I saw what I thought was a frog on the path leading
to their front door.

I'd always liked frogs. But with a sudden violence, I stepped on it.
Squashed it beneath my sandaled foot.

My uncle Richard required a span of some years to forgive me. For a
long time afterward, he thought of me as a vicious child.

And I was. At that moment, for no reason I knew then or know now,
I was vicious.

I've regretted it ever since.

ACCORDING TO BEN, who was there, my victim was probably not
a frog but a Fowler's toad—there are only two species of true toads in
Massachusetts.

Male Fowler's toads make mating calls that attract both sexes. The
male who issued the call will then try to mate with anyone who shows
up. If his chosen partner turns out to be another male, the toad will issue
a "release" call.

Informing him politely that a mistake has been made.

Years later Ben—who earns his living writing TV shows but is a brilliant visual artist, like his father before him and his daughter after—
made me a birthday card in oil pastels: the face of a toad looking at me
straight-on, with his tongue lolling out of his mouth. It bears the inscription *O darling he is OK • He is happy & in Heaven.*

It's on my wall now in a frame. Along with, I recently realized with
some surprise, landscapes by other artists that involve a total of ten more
frogs and toads.

I never set out to amass multiple pictures of these creatures—I've gathered them unconsciously.

I DON'T HUNT, as several members of my southern family do, but I've done my share of killing by accident—usually with my car, a few times with my house and its surrounding landscaping. The dead have included tarantulas, birds, a beautiful ringtail that looked a bit like a lemur, a litter of baby cottontails, a young, injured coyote who drowned in my artificial pond, and once, in the most wrenching of all those episodes, a javelina.

The javelina ran into the left front wheel of my car one day, after I'd dropped my children off at school. This wasn't in the open desert but during rush hour in northwest Tucson, where the javelina was making a lightning-fast dash across four lanes of traffic.

I pulled over and ran back to the animal, who was thrashing in pain on the road. All the cars behind me had stopped, and all the ones coming the other way, too. A few women got out of their vehicles and stood with me in the middle of the street as I called 911, shaking and incoherent. It was horrible to witness the creature's suffering, the chaotic frenzy of its distress.

I still remember the kindness of those women—we'd never met before and never would again, but they held my arms and patted my shoulder and consoled me.

I didn't mean to, I protested. I couldn't help it!

No, no, they reassured me, We saw it, the javelina came in from the side. It wasn't your fault.

At the time I thought I was talking to them. Later, on reflection, it occurred to me that I hadn't been. Or only partly.

That I'd been trying, however senselessly, to apologize to the animal herself.

As though she could understand me.

As though, to the dying, a stranger's intention meant something.

Soon sheriff's cars arrived, and the javelina dragged herself into a culvert, leaving a pool of blood on the asphalt.

The traffic started up again.

One of the deputies—a young guy with a strong New York accent—asked another if he could crawl into the culvert and shoot her.

"Nah, man," said the older cop, shaking his head. "You can't be firing off your weapon. It's a densely populated area. We gotta wait for Game and Fish."

PRIVILEGED PEOPLE OF my parents' ages—the so-called Silent Generation before the baby boomers' that was born from the Depression until the end of World War II—received instruction in Latin and Greek, civics, ethics, modern languages, drama, and the arts.

These disciplines, which teach us not only what to know but how to know—including how to discern fact from advertising, logic from illogic, and genuine debate from easy insults and takedowns—are barely taught anymore. Increasingly they're seen as frivolous, and the importance of a "liberal" or general education continues to decline.

Both of my parents were much more learned than I am. My mother, though she came from a farming family, speaks and reads three living languages plus decent Latin; in college she performed plays in ancient Greek. My father spoke or read ten, though in many of these his vocabulary skewed strongly toward the archaeological.

In German, for instance, he knew a word for "passageway so narrow only a cat could fit through it," as it pertained to the architecture of the pyramids at Giza, but not, as I discovered over a hotel breakfast with him in Bavaria, the word for "eggs."

They had an understanding of many esoteric subjects and skills that will always be ciphers to me.

Selected examples: heraldry. How to weave baskets and make pots. How to build genealogical charts called ahnentafels. Key naval battles of the Napoleonic Wars. Song-dynasty Chinese junks. The movement of antique pocket watches. Which Scottish tartans denoted which Highland clans.

How to communicate in semaphore.

A GREAT ACCELERATION of change began with the Industrial Revolution: the explosion of human numbers, the pace of information-gathering, the transformation of land and waters and atmosphere. Individuals as well as regions became more and more specialized in their labor, serving a market system structured by the arithmetic of comparative advantage and economies of scale, so that farmers grew one crop instead of many and professors taught, say, organic chemistry rather than the "natural sciences."

Our expertise became both selling point and limitation: we're now extreme-habitat specialists adapted to a particular niche, unable to make a living outside them. We receive rewards not for the social merits of what we do, but according to the market's willingness to pay for it, regardless of how opportunistic or arbitrary that willingness may be. Broader fields of knowledge or capability are seen as irrelevant to our survival.

In the United States, where government policy holds education to be far less important to the country's welfare than, for example, the continuous buildout of military capacity and weapons hardware, we're being told that we no longer need the antiquated paths to wisdom that a liberal education can confer. We have our niches and the might of our machines.

But the most powerful machines we've ever made are nuclear weapons, and those are creations of language. Minerals and plastics may be their materials, but their function is a pure artifact of alphabets and numerals arranged in patterns. The computers that target and guide the missiles, which work through variations of binary code, as well as their ability to destroy: the fission reaction of the atom bomb was a direct product of physics, whose language is math.

It was our mastery of that language that created weapons of mass destruction, as concretely as fossil fuel combustion is producing a less livable atmosphere.

In hindsight, an unfortunate error that, given the state of our physics knowledge and our enthusiasm for war-making, possibly *had* to be made.

And then could never be unmade.

About a century and a half before that, it was language that gave us internal combustion.

IN MANY COUNTRIES higher education is widely accepted as a benchmark of national success, but in the United States the rejection of learned knowledge is often seen as an expression of personal liberty. So it remains controversial—a flashpoint in cultural warfare, a signifier of elitism, and a strong determinant of political allegiance.

What used to be a healthy distrust and skepticism of authority has lately turned into a dangerous hate: hating the government is closely linked to hating all official purveyors of information, not only the media but universities and scientists and intellectuals in general.

As a result of this hatred and the systemic failures that produced it, our hostility to education is now actively separating us from a shared reality. In a 2019 poll, 61 percent of Americans couldn't name the three branches of their own government. In 2020 a National Science Foundation poll revealed that one in four of us think the sun revolves around the earth—a notion that was soundly disproved in 1543.

The same poll revealed that less than half of Americans believe humans developed from earlier animals. And in 2015 more than 40 percent of us thought human beings and dinosaurs either "probably" or "certainly" once lived on earth at the same time. The earliest evidence of the genus *Homo* dates back only about 2.8 million years, separating us from the last non-avian dinosaurs by roughly 63 million more; no mammals appear in the fossil record until those dinosaurs were gone.

But such evidence isn't persuasive if you don't believe science is real. If you suspect medical care is a conspiracy to gather your personal data and see seatbelt laws as an act of government oppression—as my children's good-hearted babysitter Pat did—chances are the fossil record won't convince you.

The amassing of facts is only one aspect of education; the ability to think critically is another. But such thinking requires receptiveness to information.

WISDOM IS HARDER to define than knowledge is—more qualitative, less quantitative—but broadly might be seen as a consistency, over time, of sound judgment. Informed by morality, spirituality, and aesthetics.

In the case study of nuclear weapons, for instance, it's fair to say that, while it was the shared knowledge and industry of a massive group of scientists that brought us the most destructive munitions ever made, it's only wisdom, along with some fear and some luck, that has kept us—so far—from the annihilation of a nuclear exchange.

But luck, like hope, is not a plan.

In the case studies of the climate and extinction crises, which like-wise were produced through the building and use of machines made by knowledge, the specter of annihilation also looms—a slower process than nuclear war, but no less dire and possibly more so. Here too, only the wis-dom of policy—the language we deploy to govern group behavior—can forestall the destruction of life support.

But more and more we reject the forms of education that confer the basic wisdom of common sense, both on our leaders and on those who follow them.

Without it we're sitting ducks for tyrants and profiteers, willing to believe whatever tales they choose to tell us—words fashioned into crude bludgeons. Willing to renounce reason for the bloodlust of vengeful chants. And the often anonymous forums for hatred and vitriol that pro-liferate on our screens.

BECAUSE WE TEND to love what we know, for us it's strangeness, not familiarity, that breeds contempt. We can embrace what we find alien in individuals and dismiss it in categories—stay homophobic in general while loving a gay child, stay racist in general despite having friends from other ethnic groups.

Fine individuals, we often tell ourselves, are the exceptions.

This holds for other animals as well. Pets, say.

Most of us don't choose to make a home devoid of pets: more than two-thirds of US households include at least one. Collectively we spend almost $100 billion a year on their care and upkeep. With pets we don't need to be persuaded into sympathy: they're near and dear. We see clearly how instinctive friendship between species can be and gain a glimpse of sentience beyond our own. As well as, often, a sense of contentment and purpose.

Critics of our commitment to companion animals like to contrast the money we spend on them with the money we fail to spend uplifting our own kind. Such comparisons make less sense as examples of actual trade-offs than as rhetorical devices—if we didn't dedicate a portion of our personal budgets to pets, there's no evidence those funds would be redirected toward charitable giving.

Still, the numbers are surprising: in the year 2018, for example, we spent $490 million on our pets' Halloween costumes alone. In order of popularity, the first four store-bought costumes for pets were pumpkin, hot dog, superhero, bumblebee.

My own children chose the bumblebee rig, size small, for our pug dog. With antennae on a headband.

Surprisingly, number five was cat. Then witch, lion, and dog.

You have to assume the selection was limited from the supply side. It's not easy to sell a four-legged version of Princess Diana. But to me the numbers suggest that—unless cats were dressed up as cats, and dogs as dogs—there were a lot of dogs out there in cat outfits. And vice versa.

We spent half a billion dollars cross-dressing our two favorite pets.

The pets did not request this expenditure.

But we insisted. We love them the way we choose to.

Yet we hesitate to extend our caretaking into the world of animals beyond. The US budget for protecting endangered species from extinction, in 2018, was less than one-fifth of the cost of pet Halloween costumes.

MINE WAS AN American family, landed in Canada when I was two from Cambridge, Massachusetts, after my father was offered a position as a professor and, for a time, museum curator in Toronto. He spent much of his energy trying to decipher Meroitic, a little-understood language used from about 300 BC to 400 AD in a part of ancient Sudan known as the Kingdom of Kush. His work on Meroitic was a form of code-breaking.

Most years he also traveled to Egypt or Sudan for a month or two on excavation projects his profession calls "digs."

My parents were cosmopolitan, I see now—a sophisticated pair, who'd met abroad while my mother was teaching English in Turkey. After I was grown up I'd gape at pictures of them as a young couple in chic fifties and sixties ensembles, my mother elegant and lovely with her long black hair piled up on top of her head, my father dashingly tall and thin and never seen in public without a suit jacket. His own black hair was swept back from his brow like Cary Grant's. Although, I was once told, on digs in Egypt the locals compared him to Anthony Perkins—an actor now known to most of us only as the murderer from *Psycho*.

But when I was small they seemed unglamorous, like most parents. In the mornings, before they'd had their coffee, they walked around blearily with that black hair flattened against their heads from sleep. I remember a housecoat my mother favored for many years, its burgundy velour grown bald and patchy from wear.

My father had his own bathroom in our basement, so humid that its wallpaper and paint peeled steadily off the walls. Their rusty stains grew till they resembled an old, sepia-toned map. The Sheetrock underneath softened and fell off in chunks, and we saw two-by-fours and darkness through the hole.

Our yard was the most overgrown yard on the block. Its grass grew so long that the old, rusting lawn mower in the garage wasn't equal to the task. And my father turned his nose up at yardwork, so in temperate weather my mother went out to the yard with a sling blade. Swung it back and forth, low.

We were abashed. Other mothers on the block didn't reap. In the neighbors' yards it was the fathers who cut the lawns, pushing loud, bright orange power mowers.

Reaping wasn't a thing. Except maybe in rock songs about suicide pacts. *Come on, baby, don't fear the reaper . . .*

But the neighbors' curious stares didn't faze my mother—she'd grown up as a peach farmer's daughter. She was a pragmatist.

MEROITIC, LIKE THE dinosaurs who didn't evolve into birds, is extinct—its last speaker died almost two thousand years ago. But a few texts are left.

In 2018, when my father had been gone for fourteen years, the largest-ever array of Meroitic stone inscriptions was found at a necropolis on the Nile, along with the ruins of numerous small pyramids over the tombs of kings and queens—a Nubian version, in miniature, of the massive Egyptian pyramids at Giza.

Code-breaking riches he had never seen.

OURS WAS A house of entropy. The benign neglect of objects. A house of thousands of books, of brimming ashtrays, and of animal hair.

For we had many pets. Cats, guinea pigs, hamsters, rabbits, mice, birds, fish.

The first cats we had were a friendly orange tabby and a bad-tempered Siamese who'd come over with my parents from Egypt. She'd lived aboard their houseboat on the Nile while a team led by my father excavated ancient sites—in a hurry, since Lake Nasser would soon flood them when the Aswan High Dam went up.

She hissed when you tried to pet her.

My personal charges were the three guinea pigs I called by fancy names: Gertrude—the matriarch who would die first and prompt me to ask about suicide—and two males, Herculaneum and Scampinello. My sister Mandy, who in her adult life would become a committed animal lover with a large menagerie of pets, had a lop-eared rabbit so heavy its paws shook her bedroom floor when she let it out of its hutch to hop around. And my brother Josh had finches our father bought him in Chinatown that he kept in a tall, hanging bamboo cage resembling a temple.

The birdcage hung over a stretch of carpet in our dining room that was moistened by a constant leak from a radiator. One day my mother found a patch of what looked like grass growing beneath the cage—our birdseed, which happened to be millet, had spilled there and sprouted.

My parents were neither handy at radiator repair nor eager to call up the trades and pay for their services, so it took many seasons for that radiator leak to get fixed. We let the millet grow.

Josh also had a goldfish he'd been given as a party favor. It lived in its wretchedly small bowl for years, refusing to give up the ghost. Only when we took pity on it in its plight, and moved it into an actual aquarium, did it finally expire.

The fish was called Sauve Qui Peut. Soaky-Poo, was the way we said it. We kids were learning French in school; our parents already spoke it.

Every Man for Himself, is the equivalent phrase in English.

We never had a dog, in my childhood home, and later my mother told me she regretted this.

People who live with dogs laugh more often than those who live with cats, studies have shown, whether at the antics of the dogs or by disposition.

We laughed a lot anyway. But we didn't go in for pack dynamics. We went our separate ways, in the house.

Like our cats.

AMONG PET OWNERS with sentimental leanings, a piece of prose called "The Rainbow Bridge" has circulated since the 1980s as a condolence for the death of a pet.

I've seen it pinned to bulletin boards. Once on a coworker's desk. Once presented to me by a hipster friend in a semi-ironic gesture.

In this well-known text, after a pet dies it gambols happily in a green meadow, restored to youth and vigor. It plays and runs with other deceased pets. There, in the waiting room of the afterlife, it misses only one joy from what came before—the presence of its master.

But the loyal animal's pining is eventually rewarded. It stands alert and gazes into the distance, for the time has come for its owner, too, to pass away.

And now the two are reunited. Never to be apart again, they cross together to the other side.

"The Rainbow Bridge" may be a piece of folk heresy, since Christian dogma doesn't invite pets into the afterlife, but public feeling tends to favor their inclusion. An old episode of *The Twilight Zone* from 1962, in which a man refuses to enter what he believes is heaven when his beloved hound is denied entry, is another piece. As it turns out, at the end of the episode, the place that offered to take him in but refused to accept his dog was hell: in the real heaven, his faithful hound is welcome.

AS A CHILD I spent most of my life in a big northern city, which was multicultural and progressive and where my father's social circle was museum and university people.

When I was in grade school, the mortgage on our modest fake-Tudor bungalow stretched my parents' means—they had three kids, after all, and lived on a professor's salary. Economies had to be made: all the milk we drank was mixed from powder that came in blue-and-white boxes too heavy for us to lift. Snack foods were strictly rationed.

Every Thursday, after my mother got back from her run to the grocery store, my brother and sister and I would scarf up the whole week's snacks in a single feeding frenzy. We'd instantly split whatever it was into three equal portions, then hunker down devouring them like jailbirds defending their food trays. We'd learned the hard way that if you left your allotment of the week's snack item in the cabinet, another sibling would consume it. Stealthily.

But in the summer, while my father stayed at home to work, my mother would squeeze the rest of us into her battered Toyota Tercel and drive down to her family's peach farm in Fort Valley, Georgia. The road trip meant McDonald's lunches and a couple of Holiday Inns with pools—both excellent scores, in our opinion—and once we reached our destination, life was swank. We'd stay with her parents, whom we called Gamma and Papa, in their rambling yellow-brick house we thought of as a mansion.

There were so many bedrooms that after we each got one of our own, there were more of them left over. Hell, you could even switch from one room to another if the first room you were given didn't suit you.

At home we had no TV at all; in Fort Valley they had HBO.

The mansion's cavernous basement had a mud floor and flooded after a heavy rain, bringing in turtles and frogs with the water. There was a shooting gallery down there, with a 500-pound bale of cotton to empty your handgun or shotgun into, and a meat cellar where Papa kept country hams, fatback, and maybe twenty sausages at a time hanging on a wire. That basement seemed to be from a different era, like my grandmother's rigid, architectural girdles.

On one edge of the ground-floor ballroom there was a wide staircase that turned and turned again as you ascended. There was a small elevator, about the size of one of the public telephone booths that adorned the city streets back then.

For Papa, who'd had his first heart attack—in a long string of them—when he was forty-two, was forbidden by his doctor to use stairs. And no room on the ground floor was acceptable to Gamma to be turned into an accessible bedroom. Out of the question! That floor consisted only of the ballroom with its grand piano, a sitting room, a library, a formal dining room, a large breakfast room, a powder room, a kitchen, a walk-in "toy closet" that held our favorite treasure trove, and a butler's pantry with a second staircase for the servants. The bare necessities.

When Papa died, Gamma would decide this opulent home was a millstone. Rather than try to sell it, she simply gave it away—to the Baptist church across the street, where she and Papa used to sing in the choir. Papa had also directed the singing in adult Sunday school and been a church deacon.

In his deep southern drawl Papa called his vertical conveyance "the 'vator," which came out sounding like *vay-duh*. We considered it an honor to be invited to go upstairs in the 'vator with him: only one of us could fit at a time. It was a wooden box, built for him by farmhands, and operated with a pull cord. Its flimsy walls trembled as it ascended, emitting a low rumble.

He was a soft-spoken, kindly man, not overly interested in the economic side of farming. He supported his family, and some of his four siblings' families, in the stock and commodities markets.

Gamma was stern by comparison—a sternness she mostly exercised with Papa rather than us, say, around the matter of his liquor consumption—but she also had a good sense of humor and shook so much when she laughed that we had to laugh too.

Sometimes, alone with us kids before bedtime, she'd shed her dress and dance around making shimmying movements that cracked us up. Wearing only her girdle and a slip.

AFTER PAPA'S RETIREMENT my uncle took over the farm. He's an excellent businessman and an expert at using the federal tax code, legally and cannily, to maximize profits. Gradually he switched over the orchards from peaches to pecans and greatly expanded the farm's land base, output, and revenue. He helped to support the extended family by selling pecans in volume to China and South Korea and Vietnam, using shipping containers whose rental was available at the Port of Savannah at rock-bottom prices. Due to the massive number of goods coming over from China and the small number going back.

My uncle did things very differently from his father, and there was tension between them over this, but he loved Papa dearly.

"He was my best friend," he told me with a hush in his voice. More than thirty years after his father's death.

Chop is relentlessly hardworking. Even now, as a senior citizen—in the wake of various illnesses and fifteen surgeries, including one for a gunshot wound to the heart that almost put an end to him—he drives through the orchards most every day, keeping tabs on what's being done, what needs to be done next, and who's doing it. He knows his workers well. There was a time when a few of them would regularly get in trouble making too merry on payday, and he was usually the one to bail them out of jail.

He speaks admiringly of his tax accountant, a force to be reckoned with. "Stephanie," he said to me recently, "you put her in front of the IRS, she's happier than a pig in slop."

He speaks of pecans fondly too, in an even deeper southern drawl than Papa had.

Expresses their requirements for optimal growth, harvest, and storage as personal preferences on the part of the nuts.

"Now your *nut*," he'll confide, as though discussing an eccentric old friend, "he doesn't like a situation where . . ."

CHOP USED TO chill our blood, when we were small, with stories of a bogeyman he called "Evil Boll Weevil." Evil lived down in the basement and had given up his former diet of cotton; now all he ate was children.

But there was a threat from above as well as below: the specter of the Skyhook. "Watch out for the Skyhook," our uncle would warn us as we ran outside to play.

The Skyhook was exactly what it sounded like—a giant hook that could descend suddenly, out of a clear blue sky, and grab a kid right out of the yard. Never to be seen again.

From below, the threat was earthly: insectoid and monstrous. From above, the threat was of a dreadful machine.

Those were the years of the Cold War.

ONCE UPON A TIME, boll weevils were the scourge of the US cotton industry. In the early 1900s their devastation of crops was one of the driving forces moving black residents of the South into northern cities in the Great Migration.

A panoply of toxic insecticides was deployed against boll weevils in the 1950s, before safer methods involving pheromone traps were devised. These pesticides are now known to be very bad for people, too. One such was parathion.

Developed by the German conglomerate IG Farben under the Nazi regime, parathion is toxic to wildlife and people alike. Exposure through skin absorption or oral ingestion causes a range of extreme reactions in the human body, up to and including brain damage and death. Via pulmonary edema and respiratory arrest.

While IG Farben exploited prison laborers from Auschwitz and other concentration and extermination camps in its factories, it also, through a subsidiary, manufactured the gas Zyklon B, which was used to kill more than a million of those prisoners in the gas chambers.

The company was shut down by the Allies after the Second World War for war crimes. But the "shutdown" involved splitting it into smaller corporate entities that still make products Americans buy in great volume every day. Including BASF and Bayer.

What was the alternative: the liquidation of valuable property?

As consumers we have short memories—we can hold grudges against people, but companies are too diffuse and multivariate to resist for long.

IF WE TOSSED and turned in our beds, complaining that we couldn't fall asleep, our mother or father might suggest counting sheep.

I figured you were supposed to see the sheep as puffy wool balls with legs, leaping over a low fence one by one, but I always got distracted trying to count them. One sheep might have a poodle cut. Another, a bum leg. One was the anxious type—would run up to the fence, then balk. The rebels would refuse to jump and hang around nibbling at clumps of grass.

So I came up with my own trick to fall asleep: I pictured a single white bird, impossibly giant, who flew over a tranquil landscape far beneath, a patchwork of meadows, rivers, and forests. I probably borrowed the image from the tale of Aladdin, who was pictured in one of my books flying on his carpet over white minarets. And Sinbad the sailor dangling from the talons of the roc, a bird who was larger than a person.

In the soft crook of one of the white bird's wings, I'd lie in a soft hollow and feel the steady movement of the wings rising and falling, the pulse of a beating heart.

From time to time, as an adult, I still thought of the bird when I couldn't get to sleep. But to feel relaxed, by then, I had to picture my small children flying with me. I couldn't leave them down there on the ground—who would watch over them?

Their father was much too busy. And preoccupied. While acting in a supervisory capacity, he'd put our one-year-old daughter on the metal roof of a shed to play. He'd typed away on his laptop while she gnawed on the cords of power tools strewn around his home study.

Next I decided that others dear to me should also have a place on the bird, and I made room for them, too.

After a while it came to resemble a living personnel carrier.

But even as I fell asleep on the bird's soft back, I could be a petty little shit. Once, when Aaron pissed me off right before bedtime, I pictured the bird as an arena for punishment.

Angrily banished him to ten feet off, there on the back of the bird. There was room, but he couldn't come close.

IN WAKING LIFE I depend on multiple machines to go about my daily business, from laptops to microwaves.

But the part of my mind that brings me sleep prefers to trust a beast.

IN PAPA'S DAYS, hundreds of cows ambled through the farm's back pastures. Mostly they belonged to other farmers and were allowed to graze there for free because Papa liked them. As he made his rounds of the peach orchards, he'd pull over in his mud-spattered Buick, get out, and say hello.

There were fences to keep the cows where they were supposed to be, and along the fences grew shrubby habitat for birds and other small, wild things. The edge effect, ecologists call it.

When my uncle took over and wished to increase efficiency, the cattle were ejected and the fences torn down. To Papa's chagrin.

Once the fences were gone, so were the shrubs and grasses that had been home to so much wildlife.

After that the orchards fell silent of birdsong. Under my uncle's astute management, they grew more profitable, too.

A large volume of pesticides and herbicides is used on our farm to maximize productivity and profits. In the year 2019 alone, for example, that single family farm used about 4,000 gallons of paraquat, 1,100 gallons of imidacloprid, 1,250 gallons of chlorpyrifos, and 500 gallons of 2,4-D amine. Among others.

Chop and his wife Brenda gave me a list of these toxic chemicals voluntarily. And trustingly, too, since they know I'm a tree hugger. The poisons are business as usual.

The nonprofit where I work has sued the government more than once over the use of each of them. Paraquat has been linked to Parkinson's disease in those who apply it, for example. Imidacloprid is dangerous to 79 percent of all federally protected endangered species, by the government's own reckoning, and chlorpyrifos to 97 percent. The chemical known as 2,4-D, which can drift for miles, was an active ingredient in Agent Orange and is a suspected cancer-causer and endocrine disruptor.

It's not just one toad I need to atone for.

"Totalitarian agriculture," is how the writer Daniel Quinn referred to the larger processes and systems that include our farm—the subsumption and obliteration, across the globe, of other lifeforms for the industrial production of human food.

Monocultures of crops have come with monopolies on the machines that bring them to harvest, too. Talking about the right-to-repair movement, which is partly a response to John Deere's production of new, highly computerized farm equipment that can no longer be serviced by the farmers themselves, Chop said to me: "Buying those vehicles was the second-worst mistake I ever made. After being a farmer."

Later he sold them off and returned to the analog machines.

When my brother and I were teenagers, we had our first jobs on the farm. I folded boxes in the packing shed and he worked in the orchards.

I learned to drive between rows of peach trees, in a pale blue Pontiac from the 1960s that had water stuck in the long, heavy doors. It sloshed audibly whenever you opened or closed them.

TO MOST OF US, cars are less like mechanisms of transit than like a moving element of our homes. Our dependence on the mobility and comfort they offer us seems inseparable from freedom: in cars we can go far, go anywhere. If we like, from sea to shining sea.

Cars feel like intimates—do so much for us, and with us, that despite their status as inanimate objects they've become beloved extensions of our bodies.

Suburban houses tend to lead, as they face the street, with large and prominent two-car garages. Their design suggests the houses' primary function is to shelter cars, with minor annexes attached to contain the cars' drivers.

And in the domestic spaces we occupy, often with our children, the children of oil live too. Petroleum products and by-products are so intricately embedded in our buildings, furnishings, tools, machines, clothes, foods, and personal care items that we've turned into a petrochemical

people. Ours is the age of oil and plastics, and the polymers derived from
the processing of fossil fuels are everywhere—so constantly touched and
used and seen that in the eye-blink of a single human lifespan they've
come to seem indispensable to our routines.

The source of these products, processed into invisibility, evades our
casual observation. We don't think, looking at a Ziploc bag: This object,
way back at the base of its chain of production, comes from masses of
ancient, dead animals called zooplankton and algae, buried under rock
and subjected to intense heat and pressure for millions of years.

We don't say to ourselves, This thing I'm putting my kid's snack mix
into was made from the bodies of the ancients.

Captured in sedimentary rock.

The oil industry is intent on turning its glut of petrochemicals into
still more single-use plastic items. In the face of a far-reaching pollution
crisis in the oceans—where those discarded, undying materials mostly
end up—the industry foresees a rich future in plastics when the use of
oil and gas for fuel is scaled down more aggressively. So a new buildout
of plants is underway in the United States, and the industry continues to
tout the recyclability of polymers and stamp reassuring numbers in small
triangles on containers.

In full awareness of the fact that, globally, only 5 or 6 percent of plastic ever gets recycled.

OUTSIDE COUNTRIES WHOSE staple export is oil and whose pov-
erty levels are high, no one else has gas as easy to buy as Americans.
Weighed against our buying power—with a few exceptions when prices
have spiked—the government keeps gas so cheap that bottled drinking
water often costs more.

No other country has as many miles of road, either. Along with cheap
gas, our roads to everywhere invite us to see our vehicles not only as recreation and status symbols but as projections of our personalities. We trick
out our trucks as signifiers of power and muscle and flash, with lift kits

and hunting lights and chrome. I saw one of these in line at a vehicle-emissions testing center, during the early COVID lockdown, with a red rear-window decal that said KILL EVERYTHING.

A joke, presumably.

But I wasn't sure.

We drive the biggest cars, requiring the most gasoline, and use more of it, per capita, than most other countries. Hold it to be self-evident that we have a sovereign right to drive whatever cars we want, as often as we want, as far as we want to.

To us the large, fast, and polluting cars we've become accustomed to—much like large and fast guns, unlimited in their power and lethality—are liberty.

We're deathly afraid it might not be available without these items.

Yet the possibility of liberty preexisted them both.

IN CIRCLES LIKE MY OWN—progressive, educated, and usually middle- or high-income—fossil fuels and their by-products are increasingly and justly being demonized. They need to be consigned to the past: on this we agree.

But maybe our profound enmeshment in the materials and lifeways they've given us needs to be acknowledged. Maybe we should allow ourselves to mourn the end of fossil fuel culture as the monumental passing it will be. To eulogize the monster that we've made in order to move on.

We lived from your death, we might say. Transmogrified your bodies into energy and designed our paths according to your lights. The ease you gave us, those patterns of convenience and effectiveness, all the invented objects in their smooth polymer perfection: sometimes these things were toys, but other times they saved our lives. Sometimes they made life possible.

Before we knew, before we could see the future, you brought us many gifts. At times they were magnificent.

You brought us a certain kind of existence, we might say, a certain kind of dream. We *had* that dream. And now the sleeping is done.

8
—

AS SENIORS IN high school in Canada, in 1985 and 1986, our grade was given the privilege of a "common room" just for us—a basement lounge with some well-used, caving-in couches, wooden tables scarred by initials and swears, and a TV.

One of my classmates, a budding performance artist who wore wire-rimmed glasses perched on his beak-like nose, scrawled a large black message across the TV screen: AMERICAN EMPIRE, it read.

It struck me as witty, at first, but he'd written it with a Sharpie that didn't seem to come off. After that, every show we watched, during our spare periods, had to be filtered through those annoying letters.

Now the only thing I remember seeing, on that artfully vandalized screen, is the explosion of the space shuttle Challenger. With its seven-person crew.

How we watched it blow up, and all aboard instantly perish, behind the words *American Empire.*

A LONG LIST of animals and plants has traveled into space in rocket ships, both in the company of human astronauts or cosmonauts and in their stead: invertebrates, mammals, birds, amphibians, reptiles, and fish. Hundreds of plants. And fungal organisms like lichen.

Among mammals, squirrel monkeys, rhesus macaques, and great apes have visited space. Iberian ribbed newts, fish called mummichogs, invertebrates known as tardigrades.

Many of the animals made journeys designed to be one-way. Laika, the famous Russian space dog, died aboard Sputnik 2 in 1957—a canine hero, it was said, who gave her life for the Soviet space quest. Her trusting face was commemorated on postage stamps and in art, sometimes encased in the transparent orb of a helmet resembling a halo. She was an angel-dog.

For decades, the line from Soviet authorities was that she'd lived for about a week. But in 2002 one of the mission scientists told the press that in fact she'd died within a few hours of takeoff, from overheating and panic.

Her capsule-coffin circled the globe more than twenty-five hundred times before disintegrating on reentry.

The early US space program preferred primates to dogs when it came to test subjects. Rhesus macaques fared especially poorly, and those given the name *Albert* were the unluckiest of all.

A macaque named Albert was the first primate astronaut in history but did not reach space. He suffocated during his flight in a V-2 rocket in 1948. Another macaque, Albert II, died when his parachute failed and his capsule slammed into the ground. Alberts III, IV, and V were also killed, with V suffering another parachute failure. Albert VI, also called Yorick, survived his flight, but expired on the ground, possibly of heat stress as he sat in his closed capsule awaiting rescue.

Even in space we've practiced animal sacrifice.

ALONG WITH SPECIES, human languages and the cultures they define are dying off at a breakneck pace. In the twentieth century alone, about four hundred disappeared, and of the remaining seven thousand, one-half to 90 percent are predicted to disappear by the end of the twenty-first.

Historically much of the loss came about through European coloni-

zation, when newly subjugated peoples were either killed off or forced
to abandon their history and speak the languages of their conquerors. In
the Indian boarding-school era in the United States, which only ended
when I was about ten, native children were taken away from their parents by force and compelled to abandon not only their families but
also their traditions and words. "Kill the Indian, save the man," was an
early catchphrase.

Sometimes it was literal—in Canada, similar schools have recently
been covered in the news as the sites of discoveries of mass child graves.
More than four thousand children died in the "care" of those residential
schools, the last of which closed in 1996.

Now the loss of languages often occurs as the result of a fast-moving,
postcolonial tsunami of trade and development—though to call our
times "postcolonial" obscures the fact that the United States still runs
much of the globe through far-reaching economic domination backed
by the force of arms. Our country retains about eight hundred military
bases around the world and spends more on its "defense" than the next
ten nations combined.

As the European colonizers liquidated native cultures and
languages—destroying them, in cases such as the Mayan codices, with
a ferocity that included burning down libraries that held the lion's share
of a whole civilization's written literature—they erased a heritage of
storytelling in which nature and other animals were interlinked with
the human world. And replaced those stories with their own, in which
white people, and their desires and agency, were not only dominant
but monolithic.

To what degree remaining traditional cultures have the ability, much less the will, to prevent their languages' extinction is an
open question.

When the first gun that could fire multiple shots was mass-
produced—an honor that goes to the revolver invented by Samuel Colt,
who patented his .45 in 1836—the extinction of large numbers of traditional societies, along with their painstakingly accumulated knowledge of
the natural world, may have become a practical inevitability.

"God created man, Sam Colt made them equal," ran the most famous early ad slogan for the Colt revolver.

It's now available to gun lovers on T-shirts and bumper stickers.

IN *THE RAGGED EDGE OF THE WORLD*, journalist Eugene Linden described his encounters with Indigenous people living at the boundaries between nature and development, history and modernity.

No matter how much tribal elders, activist youth, and even well-meaning outsiders may wish for the preservation of the old ways, he noted, hunters tend to gravitate, in the end, toward the most effective tools. Wherever they find them and whenever they can afford to buy or trade for them.

Because after all—as an anthropologist told Linden while they were discussing the Penan people of Borneo, albeit in politer words—hunting with blowpipes is fucking hard.

This is the case with pursuits outside hunting, as well: the machines of the modern are undeniably handy, bestowing access and capacity. Once the products of industrial technology reach formerly isolated peoples, their assimilation, and the disappearance of their lexicon and ancient patterns of knowing, tends to follow.

Some argue that this idea of the inevitability of cultural decline is itself a pernicious story—that it offers a grand permission to modern economic colonizers to plunder and supersede. That it's a simple extension of the deadly logic of capital, where domination and expropriation, rather than constituting crimes against humanity, are unavoidable off-shoots of progress.

PEOPLE WITH CATARACTS in their eyes have described them to me as blurred spots in their vision. And at the dawning of our awareness of the climate threat, its danger to the balance of the biosphere was a bit like that: a slight distortion at the edge of our awareness. A dark floater in our field of view.

So when we began to hear that the way we lived was setting our life-support systems on a perilous trajectory, we failed, for decades, to come to grips with the dire prediction. After all, there had *always* been doom-sayers, the climate deniers liked to remind us—alarmist whack-jobs beating the drums of dread.

Attention-seekers, cult leaders, delusional prophets.

They'd never been right before.

9

IN DECEMBER OF 1968, when I was about three weeks old, Apollo 8 circled the moon. From lunar orbit an astronaut took pictures of the home planet, one of which came to be called *Earthrise*.

Released by NASA for public view, within days the photo had been printed in black and white on the front page of sixty-odd newspapers across the country. But the color image that's now so iconic was first seen widely in *Life* magazine's New Year edition, along with verse written by the poet James Dickey.

"Behold," he wrote, "the blue planet steeped in its dream."

Some seven months later I watched the moon landing of Apollo 11 from a playpen. I don't recall this, of course, but there are photographs. It was a small step and a giant leap, they said.

Now we've deposited robot cars on the surface of Mars and sent Voyagers 1 and 2 beyond the heliopause, where solar winds die down, to enter the no-man's-land of interstellar space. We've seen pictures streaming in from the James Webb telescope that show us carbon dioxide on a planet far away and a million galaxies in a grain of sand.

We still listen to the story about conquering the stars. Marvelous machines seem to be moving us toward omniscience, and on-screen future humans continue to cross the galaxy as masters of the universe.

But meanwhile a second story, also told by science, has risen to undermine the first. It says our way of life is not a triumph anymore but a mass suicide. That the grid of our society—with its far-flung suburbs around the hubs of distant cities, its sprawling homes, its coal- and gas-fired power plants, its fast, smooth roads that give us, when we drive on them, a stirring sensation of self-reliance—is tending swiftly deathward.

In the new math of carbon, it says, our vehicles are destroyers. The meat and seafood that we eat too much of and extravagantly discard (in the United States, the global leader in food waste, we throw up to 40 percent of our food supply into landfills, our third-largest source of methane emissions). The clothes we wear. The coffee and alcohol and milk we drink, all of which have outsize footprints. Our garbage. Our lights. Our ways of keeping warm in the winter and cool when it's hot outside. The jets we fly in for our jobs and vacations.

This new story threatens the way we live, in the rich parts of the world—and in the poorer parts, the way we want to live. And it's being told by the very same authorities who first supplied us with our excellent machines, the same purveyors of knowledge who promised that those excellent machines would lift us up and save us.

Now they're singing a different tune: those cars and planes and power plants will be our undoing.

No one prepared us for this ugly reversal of myth. The stories that underpin a culture can't be jettisoned from one cold moment to the next.

The scientists seem to have forgotten the rules of storytelling. Or to be stubbornly ignoring them.

Naturally we prefer the first story. The second lacks a happy ending.

So denial is a natural response. Many among us have decided that the scientists, once firmly ensconced in our pantheon of heroes, are now the villains of the piece.

DENIAL ERODES OVER TIME, and as it decays we begin to feel trapped by those ominous predictions of the future, descending like falling ash.

We feel caught in a trap too heavy to push open from the inside. And find ourselves yearning for a magical intervention—some miracle of will and cooperation that's hard to believe in. A miracle that will defy the inertia of institutions, where the corrupt become honest and the unmoving suddenly move.

Failing that, it seems to us, a dark age is on its way.

Even if we do our level best, we're told, more losses are inevitable. Unknown yet in their details but as sure as the passing of time.

So it will be darker for our children than for us, is what we fear. And darker for their children than for them.

Darker still for the beasts.

RECREATIONAL DRUGS WEREN'T laced with fentanyl, when I was in my twenties, and thus had less potential to be instantly lethal than they do now—unless you shot them up with shared needles, for it was the early era of AIDS.

I didn't seek them out often, since I spent most of my spare time writing, but at the occasional party, when a generous acquaintance saw fit to offer me a little coke, acid, meth, or Ecstasy, I typically said yes, thank you. And then showed such a lack of self-restraint that friends had to hold me back when I teetered at the edge of tenement rooftops.

I'd chase the drugs with so many beers, over the course of a night, that it's surprising I didn't also suffer the effects of alcohol poisoning.

Moderation has never been my strong suit.

Before I had children, I gave up those risky behaviors. By choice, but also by lack of proximity.

Now I have plenty of other bad habits—mostly consumer vices that, far from being illegal, are enthusiastically sanctioned by the state and the marketplace. Packages arrive at my house from halfway across the world, encased in cardboard and plastic. Wine is purchased by the crate. If I have a chance to smoke socially, I eagerly take it.

I used to have one big habit, as Iggy Pop has said. *Now I've got twenty little, perverted, self-destructive habits.*

There are only two ways you could get me to go without the vices I still possess.

One, you could make it the law. Impose penalties for violations.

Or two, you could treat me like a child.

And move those vices and conveniences beyond my reach.

In the realm of sacrificing pleasures, folks like me, who consume too much simply because it's possible and easy, are the norm.

People like me need rules.

LONGEVITY, AMONG WARM-BLOODED animals, appears to be related to how many neurons a species has in its cerebral cortex. This number, according to a recent study out of Vanderbilt University, is a far better predictor of long life than body size. Parrots and corvids live longer than we do, relative to their basal metabolic rate, because they have more of these neurons. Which seem to exist as a fixed allotment from birth, not changing or growing over time.

Still, in possessing many of these neurons, *Homo sapiens* has a long childhood and a long adolescence—longer than many other species. And we use that extended period of growth to understand ourselves as social beings.

As we grow up, our self-awareness increases. Emerging from beneath the umbrella of parenting, we struggle to understand where we fit into the mosaic of other people. Assess whether they mean what they say, what they want and why they want it—their intentions and aversions. We learn who to trust and who to keep at arm's length.

Our adolescent years are an engagement with the development of mind-reading: acquiring the skill of anticipating the behaviors of others of our kind.

And our level of mastery of that skill is one determinant—after demographic factors we can't control, such as the ZIP codes we're born in, the sex we're born as, and the color of our skin—of personal success.

But we retain blind spots.

AS A YOUNG ADULT I was quite certain that I had supreme authority on the subject of myself. It took a string of failures of perception for me to understand that, even on that subject, I wasn't always a reliable witness.

A close friend of mine likes to tell an anecdote about how I once prized what I saw as honesty above kindness.

It happened one night, when we were both in our twenties, that my friend was broken up with and miserable.

With a bottle of wine in hand, I went over to her Brooklyn apartment, sat beside her on a couch, and listened to her accounting of the sad event. I hugged her and patted her knee. Went out to get more wine. Came back and patted her knee some more.

She was hard to comfort: after years by herself, often suffering from depression, she'd finally found the person she wanted to be with. And then he'd chosen to leave.

All she was looking for was sympathy. I didn't know what to say. But was determined to offer reassurance. Along with, of course, the existential honesty I prized.

I took her by the hand and said gently, Hey, it's going to be OK. It won't really matter, after a while. Because, you know, in the end we all die alone.

Later that man came back—they got married and are still married today. Still, she's never forgotten my poor skill as a consoler.

All of us have personal blind spots. But whole cultures do, as well. And those are even harder to see from within. With the might and legitimization of institutions behind them, even the radical violations of genocide and slavery have gained the consent of millions.

We live inside culture less consciously than we live inside our personalities—an authority so broad and formless we can rarely pick out its features from the landscape, rarely see the forest for the trees. Can't discern where its dictates end and selfhood begins.

Or whether such a dividing line exists.

In hindsight, the blind spots of cultures are easy to identify.

In day-to-day time, less so.

IN CHINA, DURING what was called the Great Leap Forward between 1958 and '62, the regime of Chairman Mao Zedong directed its citizens to carry out mass actions called the Four Pests Campaign. This was an effort to rid the land of nuisance animals.

One of the "pests" was a small, common bird: the sparrow. Those sparrows needed to be eliminated, Mao decreed. They stole and ate the people's rice.

The populace did his bidding. Soldiers, students, civil servants—under the banner of Kill Sparrows, they banged on pots and pans relentlessly, until, as the story goes, the sparrows, exhausted by their inability to alight on trees and branches, fell dead from the sky.

Wherever their nests were found they were destroyed, the eggs smashed. Throughout the country birds perished.

The Great Leap Forward set steel production as the economic goal, following Stalin—though mostly lumps of brittle, useless cast iron were produced—and forced peasants to abandon private food production. Less land was planted for grain, and on that land crop yields plummeted; what food was still produced was commandeered by the central authorities.

A famine took hold that lasted for three years and resulted, according to scholars, in 36 million to 45 million human deaths.

Even official Chinese reports, which treat the episode as a natural disaster rather than a series of policy mistakes, admit the toll was close to 20 million. Cannibalism occurred among families, with children and parents eating each other's bodies as tens of millions starved.

For their part, all along the sparrows had been doing more good than harm. They'd eaten the insects that plagued the rice paddies. After they were removed, locust populations exploded.

A regrettable oversight, the blind spot about the sparrows. And the steel.

And the tens of millions.

10

—

THE GULF OF OMAN, in the Arabian Sea, contains the earth's largest marine dead zone. Scientists confirmed this in 2018 using underwater robots. The dead zone—a term that refers to low-oxygen waters—extends over most of the Gulf, an area roughly the size of Florida or Scotland.

On the open ocean these dead zones are being caused by warming. Along the coasts, agricultural runoff and sewage drive the problem. When low oxygen levels begin to suffocate the fish living there, they can swim away—though whether they're able to find good habitat elsewhere is an open question.

But organisms that can't move die. And the Gulf of Oman turns green with algae for several months a year.

Globally marine dead zones are growing in size and number. Since 1950 the area of zones with zero oxygen has quadrupled, while the number of low-oxygen sites near coastlines has increased tenfold.

Beyond this "hypoxia," in the continuum of oxygen depletion, lies anoxia, when oxygen levels reach zero. In the past, when ocean anoxia has occurred on a planetary scale, it has coincided with mass extinction. And a warming climate.

The first mass extinction, known as the Ordovician-Silurian, happened 450 million years ago. The Late Devonian extinctions about 360 million years back. The P-T event, or Great Dying, about 250 million years ago, extinguished 90 percent of the planet's species.

There's a mass extinction about every hundred million years.

The extinction of the non-avian dinosaurs, 66 million years ago, was different—almost certainly caused by the Chicxulub impactor, an asteroid or meteor that struck what's now called Mexico.

So mass extinction—as those who choose to deny its importance like to argue—*is* a part of nature. Undoubtedly. And at least once before, it was meteoric. Set into motion by a cataclysmic and sudden event.

Far more typically, extinction has come about through the extremely slow, rolling shifts of physical systems that phase out old lifeforms and repopulate the earth anew. Over deep time, repeatedly, the planet has reshaped the thin, life-holding layer of its surface. And those who inhabit that surface, from trilobites to dinosaurs.

We've lived in a world with mammoths and saber-tooth cats and giant sloths, although we don't remember it. Along with hundreds of other great beasts. Drove most of them to extinction by our own hand, most probably, though some still resist this Pleistocene "overkill" hypothesis. Paleontologists are busily working to reconstruct the histories of these creatures, but reconstruction is not memory.

And, after the Pleistocene, we've lived in a world without them.

But we've never lived in a world where millions of species have disappeared virtually overnight.

SOMETIMES IT SEEMS miraculous that we can conceive of the distant past, imagining the world before our kind. And after. That we can describe even the kinds of beasts with whom we never lived, who were here so long ago. Rebuild their bodies out of fragments of bone and information.

It used to make me shiver, when I was young, thinking of the depths of space and time. How we can see into that deep time, digging into the earth or casting into the sky, but never live across it.

I shivered at the sublime paradox back then and sometimes I still do—a vision of the infinite, seen through our finite eyes.

RING THE BELLS

1
—

SOME SAY ALL narratives are lies.

Fiction admits this freely, delighted to shed the burden of reporting facts and deal instead in character and metaphor. By its nature it forfeits only audience, since it has to be chosen to be read—and has to seem understandable to be chosen in the first place. Made-up stories are popular in their screen forms, but when it comes to print, a 2021 Pew Research poll suggested, half of US adults are unable to read a book at even an eighth-grade level.

Polls can be dismal messengers, of course, with findings that often strain credulity. They also try to tell us, for instance, that almost half of all American college graduates never read another book, either fiction or nonfiction, after they graduate.

This doesn't mean they don't read at all. Only that they don't read books.

In the news and current-events economy, beyond the self-aware fantasies that a minority of us still choose to write and read, the task of stories is to convey the real. There the stakes are higher and narratives skew toward reduction, with shorthand and symbols in the place of long blocks of printed text. And good and bad guys cast in bold relief to capture our attention.

Outside the fact-checking circuits of journalism, in the outpouring of narrative content that social media has enabled, individuals once relegated to the margins have become powerful vectors of story. There the pull toward oppositional drama is strong—so that the line between the imagined and factual is now so blurred that large segments of the US population adhere to conspiracy theories such as QAnon, which has also spread to other countries.

Fanciful tales like those told by QAnon have the advantage of turning daily life into a thrilling soap opera that features images of vampirical predation and child sexual abuse. They have to claim to be nonfiction: they couldn't go viral without making an assertion of factuality. Fictional vampire stories are already fully commodified, spent and abundant in the marketplace: the fresher commodity is the extremist real.

To feel urgent and threatening, the legends pin themselves to politics, where villains wield social and economic power. The vampires of the extremist real have outwardly bland faces, a centrist politics, and the weight of institutions behind them.

The mainstream position of these vilified establishment figures—say, Hillary Clinton or Barack Obama or George Soros—is a necessary element: minor players with bit parts don't make for credible or useful antagonists. To the purveyors of the extremist real, Noam Chomsky is of little interest.

At its best, art is an antidote to such dangerous abuses of language. Novels, poems, songs, images, and passages of philosophy unspool in a way that wishes to illuminate the ambiguities and complexities of experience.

And reflects on the first and last condition of the word—how the ongoing, eternal failure to articulate a perfect truth is itself the crisis and terrible beauty of language.

TO YEARN FOR recognition is to want to stamp yourself into posterity: into the now of a society, but also its *then*—its future past. As a teenager I shared this wish with many others. How could I *be* something?

I thought of acting, maybe. That was a popular choice. Then I played a saucy French maid in a high school musical and quickly realized I was a terrible actor—wooden and self-conscious. Also, not gorgeous enough to be on movie posters.

I next thought of singing opera and pursued this goal for several years. I had a loud voice but lacked the patience to study musicology. It seemed a lot like math. Plus, in opera you were called upon to act.

Oddly, rock star never occurred to me. Neither did athlete or entrepreneur or politician. And platforms like YouTube and Instagram were not available.

As a devoted reader of fiction, I'd settled on writing by the time I went to college. It came with a pleasing independence of process, unlike acting or singing, and had an expansiveness to it: you could be playful or serious in your inventions. And weren't instantly subject to the whims and management of others.

It would take some time for me to see that this pursuit was not a fast road to recognition. Or maybe any road at all.

But by then I was lost. I'd already come to love it.

A FAMOUS LINE from a letter written by the French novelist Gustave Flaubert has been quoted to me more than once to help assuage my conscience: *Be settled in your life and as ordinary as a bourgeois, in order to be fierce and original in your works.*

Flaubert was a bourgeois who hated the bourgeoisie, self-hating and self-elevating at once. But he was onto something.

From the comfort of a middle-class arrangement, writers—in pursuit of whatever aesthetic end we purport to be seeking—can politely absent ourselves from other avenues of participation in civic or social struggle.

Our art is the gift we offer you, my friends. Whether you asked for it or not.

A more ingenious excuse for artists' self-indulgence and political apathy has never been devised.

WHEN I WAS sixteen I took a philosophy class taught by a lively young man several of us had crushes on: we found him so charming and magnetic that we were even willing to overlook his lavishly uncool mustache, a style relic of the seventies that seemed to be stubbornly occupying his face.

He encouraged us to be bold in our lives and intellects, and to that end allowed me to explore the work of the Marquis de Sade, whose name is now the root of the word *sadism*, denoting cruelty for the purpose of sexual gratification.

In retrospect I'm surprised that the teacher and I got away with this choice of reading material at the venerable institution that housed us: Sade's writings, which feature graphic and gleeful descriptions of pedophilia, necrophilia, rape, coprophagy, bestiality, infanticide, and torture, wouldn't fly as subject matter in any high school I'm familiar with today.

And although only a few years later I'd find myself working in the "adult entertainment" industry, I've still never encountered harder-core print pornography than what Sade came up with back in the 1780s. *The 120 Days of Sodom*, which I focused on for my philosophy project, was his most extreme book, written while he was locked up in the Bastille and only published more than a century later.

A dissipated aristocrat and libertine, Sade could never be accused of separating his life from his work. He wasn't a comfortable bourgeois. Arrested more than once on charges of mistreatment of women and sodomy, he spent many of his years in prison and died in an asylum at the age of seventy-four, poor, obese, and with a teenage maid for a girlfriend— one he'd been sleeping with since she was at most fourteen.

His recent veneration as a French national treasure is itself a complicated study in cultural values.

In my final presentation on his ideas, I passed around a handout with black blocks over whole sentences where the teacher had redacted the most explicit passages. It looked like a declassified document that posed a threat to national security.

But *I* had read the passages, of course.

Sometimes, when I come across discussions of literary censorship or book-banning in schools, I recall those violent and sexual texts in a granular detail that's attached to very few of my other memories. I doubt that I'll ever dispel the images they imprinted—Sade's archetypal depravities would never fully leave my mind.

But neither would the mad extravagance of his gesture: the choice to write them down.

DURING COLLEGE I spent a year at a university in the city of Montpellier, in the south of France, and half of another at the London School of Economics.

In Montpellier I was placed in the home of a local family for the year. I was a boarder, nothing more, and mostly ran into them in the kitchen. My room was at the end of a long hall on the second floor, with a spacious balcony. I sat out there in the evenings and wrote poetry in French, inspired by some surrealists I'd been reading.

I believed my French poetry was quite fine. Had a hunch that, much like Vladimir Nabokov, who could write with fluid brilliance in a tongue that was not his first, I might be a secret genius. (A forensic analysis of the texts suggests otherwise.)

The house was outside the city, and I had to take two buses to get to campus. Out on the balcony, in the evenings, I'd gaze across the quiet countryside. It seemed like a box seat in a theater: flotation in the dark. On cloudless nights the stars came out, and the blinking lights of aircraft tracked across the sky.

On my balcony I was elated by the vastness of the universe, the conundrum of its edges. Physicists said it was expanding—but where to? Was there an end to the universe? If so, what lay beyond that end?

And if there was no edge, if it went on forever, how was that possible? What did forever look like, for the universe?

It was 95 percent dark energy and dark matter, they were telling us. Dark energy and dark matter that we didn't yet comprehend.

LIKE MOST OF my writer friends, I feel awkward at political protests. Their motivational slogans, along with other trappings of crowd behavior, make us feel itchy even when we believe in a cause. Slogans are reductive and rhetorical while our job is the opposite: nuance and subtlety.

In my twenties, during a brief foray into labor advocacy, I was persuaded to dress up as a human-sized strawberry for a demonstration over the health and welfare of farmworkers. The protest was staged outside Dean & DeLuca, a luxury food store in downtown Manhattan that, many years later, would file for bankruptcy during the COVID-19 pandemic.

I was relieved to be encased in my strawberry outfit—which smelled strongly of stale body odor—because it covered my face. This meant my fellow protesters couldn't see me grimace as we shouted out, "The people! United! Can never be defeated!"

I chanted along with the crowd thinking, Well, but they can, sadly. And often they are.

THE FINGERS OF language touch all the projects and projections of humanness. Words can murder or save, justify evil or define the ideal, bring us laughter and elegies alike, the lies of advertising and the neatness of arithmetic. Marriage and divorce. Skyscrapers and cruise missiles.

Beginning to write fiction, and being young, I liked to think I could do something new with storytelling, if I worked hard enough. It was important to me to try to innovate. Possibly formally, like the stylists I admired—say, Samuel Beckett or Virginia Woolf. Or possibly in content, like the iconoclasts—Baudelaire, maybe, or even Sade.

The libraries and stores were already full of books, so full that when I entered them I felt something like vertigo, discouraged by the threat of redundancy—the sinking feeling that, however hard I struggled to invent, I'd always be duplicating.

Later I'd recognize the futility of my goal of newness. Since even to begin to comprehend what constitutes the new you need to know the

old. The bottomless history of the written, its endless volumes and lexi-
cons. I could read for a hundred lifetimes and never know what already
existed when I began.

And at a certain point, if you're a writer, you have to stop reading
and write instead. I carry an internal library with me everywhere, but it's
smaller than that of many other people I know—a library in miniature.
Like the ones erected by community-minded readers on neighborhood
corners that contain a random selection of donated material, from dog-
eared romances to detective stories to automotive manuals. Sometimes
with an odd knickknack thrown in: I've seen a plastic peacock and a dis-
favored candlestick, bulbous with wax drippings.

Meanwhile the written history is constantly expanding. Like the universe. Or entropy. And can never be caught or captured.

So that newness, like happiness, is a chimera.

What *can* be caught is the thrill of making something. In writing,
for me, it occurs in the rare moments when I come to feel the words
are reaching for a gulf of experience beyond them. A conjuration of the
unsayable—a mysticism of fragments, an ecstasy of ideas.

Writing is an act of faith. Like all beloved acts.

BECAUSE OF THE homogenizing qualities the written word has taken
on—particularly English, which has now claimed so much of the globe
as its patrimony—it's sometimes criticized by those who believe that
oral storytelling is a kinder and more organic form. This criticism is performed, often, in writing, an irony that doesn't escape the scholars and
writers who practice it.

The desirability and realism of progress and infinite growth, they say,
is a pernicious propaganda we believe is true—and, in its ironclad ortho-
doxy, not unlike the stories of fundamentalist faiths whose adherents
deny the value of alternate belief systems.

Cultures cleave to their overarching stories without reflection or
interrogation, and individuals cleave to their cultures the same way. Only

in situations of extreme chaos or social breakdown is the falseness of a cultural narrative made manifestly visible.

Chaos like flooded cities, you might think. Raging wildfires. Frequent famines and swiftly migrating pandemics, many of them "zoonotic"— originating in our mistreatment of wildlife and destruction of its habitat.

Cascades of extinctions.

But even there, the empires that contain those cities and wildfires and blown-down orchards or failing crops have been able to reassure us, so far, that our central story is still true.

For these events are outliers, they keep insisting. We can stay on the road to growth, they tell us. We can continue to act exactly as we do now.

The telling of our monomythic story of progress and triumph—the superstory that captures us all—will brook no interruption.

Until the very minute when we find ourselves, surprised into speech-lessness, standing among the ruins.

Led into a dead end by a story that proved untrue.

THE EARLIEST WRITING SYSTEMS were composed, in large part, of pictures of beasts and plants: Egyptian and Cretan hieroglyphs, cune-iform in Sumeria, the Olmec and Maya scripts of Mesoamerica. Those systems came into use around the time of the Bronze Age, though—like our own golden age of oil technology—it wasn't a bronze age for everyone.

In visual art the beasts were equally ascendant. The cave artists at Las-caux, around seventeen thousand years ago, took great pains with their work—brought in pigments from hundreds of miles away to do it. Las-caux and Chauvet and the other ancient art-decorated caves discovered in Europe, Asia, India, and Indonesia (the world's oldest cave drawings are on the island of Sulawesi) do not depict landscapes.

There are imprints of human hands, many of them believed to be those of women or children. There are a few geometric shapes.

But the majority of the pictures are of four-legged creatures.

Our earliest drawings, like the glyphs that later morphed into words, were images of the beasts.

When the glyphs receded, replaced by abstracter symbol alphabets, the creatures remained in ghostlier forms. Like metaphor. And the music that mimicked birdsong.

Language was made of animals. As was art.

THE SPLENDOR OF Indian peacocks, whose extravagant tails of green and gold fan out so wide their bodies seem like an afterthought, is a stark case of what biologists call "sexual dimorphism"—when the males and females of a species look strikingly different. With peafowl the contrast between the resplendent males and dull-brown hens strikes us as almost laughable.

In birds an obvious dissimilarity between the sexes is common—though rarely so extreme as with peacocks and peahens—but sexual dimorphism is found in many other groups of animals and plants as well.

Humans place great value on the body differences between our own sexes, whose biological distinctions have functioned through the ages to justify systems of male dominance and female subservience.

Yet in *Homo sapiens*, sexual dimorphism is low.

AFTER COLLEGE, FOR two and a half years, I had a job correcting the grammar and spelling in porn magazines. (Along with others, including the gun magazine I mentioned earlier.)

At the time I couldn't find other work—I was summarily, and probably deservedly, rejected for a housecleaning gig and fired from an assistant position that required me to wash a TV producer's white Jaguar. I moonlighted as a food server and an incompetent clown at corporate picnics.

This was in Beverly Hills, California, where I only secured the editing job because a roommate's acquaintance happened to be leaving her position and was kind enough to shoehorn me in.

What I discovered at the magazine offices—besides the obvious: a barrage of images of naked women good for nothing but sex—was the spreading osmosis of their degradation and subordination, a leakage of contempt for women and girls into a cynical debasement of other-than-white-maleness in general. (Or maybe the leakage had gone the other way: which category of hatred was the ur-hatred, the origin point of all the category hatreds, was murky to me then and remains so today.)

There were rudimentary racist jokes in the magazine's pages, along with sexist ones, and a "humor" section I edited ran pictures of women eating from dog food bowls on all fours. This elevated our readership above women and other animals in one fell swoop—a punchline that was only a punch.

On the surface our flagship magazine, *Hustler*, seemed to be selling images of women's bodies, but beneath that surface its product was clearly the celebration of male anger.

Many convicts followed the magazine faithfully and wrote highly intimate letters to us, as its editors, and to the models on the pages. One of these convicts was a serial killer who was both a reader and a subject: he'd been the focus of an "investigative" feature we ran on his life and crimes.

Serial killers were fashionable in pop culture then, as they still are, with female pen pals lining up to gain their favor and become their conjugal-visit girlfriends or wives. Or more recently, young boys on Tik-Tok aspiring to emulate the stylings of fictional serial-killer antiheroes like Patrick Bateman, the star of *American Psycho*.

But the telling of the serial killer's story, in our magazine, was also a logical extension of its mission. As a crucible of rage.

The killer was Richard Ramirez, convicted of thirteen murders as well as several assaults involving rape and torture—the Night Stalker, he was dubbed. With a certain romantic flare.

Ramirez was unrepentant. When the verdict on him came down, he said, "Big deal. Death always went with the territory. See you in Disneyland."

He called my boss from death row to complain about a typo in the feature (which had been my oversight, as the copy editor). I was duly rebuked. And an apology was offered to the serial killer for my proofreading mistake.

As it happened, Ramirez, who claimed to have been inspired in his evildoing by Satan, was never executed. He lived out his natural life on death row, from which abode he would marry a fangirl, who happened to be a magazine editor, in 1997.

A series of appeals kept him alive for some twenty years, after that phone call, until he died of cancer in 2013.

THE MAGAZINE-PUBLISHING STAFF had a workmanlike commitment to misogynist aggression, which it packaged dutifully and sometimes with a rueful resignation—much as you might do in a factory that churns out toilet plungers or kitty litter. A demand existed; we were there to meet that demand.

But day to day, as in any factory, there was ambient abjection and a sense of powerlessness. One colleague slept in his office and rarely bathed, carrying with him a fug of body odor; another masturbated with free sex toys sent in for him to review

For a while I rode a bicycle to work and, since there were no bike racks, had to store it propped against the front of my desk. One of the men I worked with used to wander into my office and caress the bike's smooth vinyl seat as he spoke to me, on some trivial pretext, in long, dull sentences. After a lingering stroke of the seat, he would lift his fingers to his nose. And inhale.

Despite this, he never registered as much of a threat—barely seemed to notice he was sniffing his fingers right in front of me. He was neither unintelligent nor afflicted with any formal challenges, but still appeared to exist in a zone outside clarity, a gray smudge of truncated self-awareness. He puttered around the office constantly, making dutiful daily rounds, looking for people to talk to and grateful when he found them.

Once he homed in on his quarry and began to speak, he appeared to have no goal for the conversation. He'd roll out a set of remarks so self-evident and bland it was impossible to think of a response to them.

He'd stand in the doorway of our office delivering a slow, soft oppression of boredom while we typed away at our keyboards. After some time elapsed, we'd feel compelled to leave the office. Embarked on a bathroom or printer run, we'd brush past the unmoving obstacle of his body as though it was furniture, hoping our absence would dislodge him.

He must have been lonely. But his way of seeking companionship made it impossible.

For he was one of those people who can't tell a story to save their life.

IT'S HARD TO KNOW where the talent for telling stories comes from. But those who tell them best tend to be those who aren't afraid of letting down their guard—of exposing the chinks in their armor.

My uncle Chop isn't a voracious reader, outside military history—certainly he hasn't read any of my books—but he knows how to hold the attention of a room. Tells anecdotes with a vigor and sense of dramatic timing that makes shyer people like me fall silent. Some are extended, with baroque flourishes, others short and pithy.

Driven too hard by work, stress, and sleeping pills a few years ago, he parked his truck in a pecan orchard one morning, aimed a gun at his heart, and pulled the trigger.

He was found in time and survived. It's surprisingly hard to shoot yourself fatally in the heart, a surgeon friend told me.

But afterward he looked like a different man—thinner and older.

After some months of recovery, he says, he took up his former routines again and one day, at lunchtime, headed into a local fast-food joint.

The woman behind the counter, whom he'd known for years, keyed in his order politely but didn't recognize him.

"It's me," he said. Grinning, I'm sure. "Chop Evans!"

"Mr. *Evans?*" she said. She peered at him more closely. "Heavens. What happened to *you?*"

"Well, now, I shot myself!" he said.

AT *HUSTLER* I shared an office with two other copy editors, also in their early twenties, who'd become my friends. It had wall-to-wall carpet, and when there was no work coming in we'd lock the door and take catnaps under our desks.

I was fast asleep beneath mine when I got a call on my office phone from a small press offering to publish my first novel, with a modest advance. Euphoric and half disbelieving, I bounded through the corporate hallways as though I'd won the lottery.

And I had.

After that, I left as soon as I could. Went to grad school to study conservation while I waited for my book to be published.

I'VE STRUGGLED TO write about the other animals in fiction. In stories intended for adult readers, they present difficult technical hurdles. As soon as you write dialogue for them—a rare gambit for good reason—you're turning them into puppets in human costume. The gesture slips into farce or ridicule.

Even an internal monologue, when delivered on behalf of a nonhuman animal, is in most cases an awkward belaboring.

Certain shamans, I've read, can inhabit an animal mind, but those of us with plainer, less transformative capacities meet with a truncated failure. Of both art and verisimilitude.

On the other hand, if you don't give an animal the gift of speech or thought, in a story, you turn it into decor. The animal is not a character, then—a creature with agency and awareness—but a living accessory whose role is chiefly to reflect the tastes and emotions of the human characters around it.

The other animals aren't easy protagonists, in fiction.

Yet I feel their absence keenly.

So I seek out the company of beasts—in language, if not in the flesh—in my day job.

AFTER GRAD SCHOOL I lived for three years in Manhattan, working as an environmental grant writer. Then, at the beginning of January in 1999—a month I always found barren and depressing in the city, except on the rare occasions when snow fell and turned it all into a white fairyland—I left to spend the winter in southern Arizona.

Tucson was the headquarters of my favorite conservation group, a small outfit called the Center for Biological Diversity run by a handful of activists who'd formerly been part of a biocentric movement called Earth First! [sic]. I'd read email bulletins from its director regularly, in my sustainably furnished grant-writing office in the Flatiron District.

The emails consisted of lists of the things the small group had done every week on behalf of endangered animals and plants and the places they lived in: a concise, unflagging detail of practical action using science and law.

I quit my grant-writing position, said a temporary goodbye to my boyfriend of seven years, Randolph, my best friend Jenny, and my cousin Ben, and flew to the Southwest. I was hoping that by interning for the small group for free, I could prove useful and garner some paid freelance assignments—bring my work back to New York with me. Writing and editing could be done anywhere.

But in the wide night skies of the desert, I could see the stars again, as I had from my balcony in the south of France. The celestial sphere, unobscured by city lights and tall buildings.

Towering clouds loomed and billowed—great, anvil-shaped white-and-purple monoliths that seemed to brood over the land below. The moon was huge, often a deep orange, and on clear nights I could make out a faint, bristling field I'd never seen before, so many stars they seemed to wash together like a brushstroke. This was the Milky Way, our own spiral galaxy: a white blur across the dark.

At the center of which, we now know, lies a supermassive black hole. With a mass four million times greater than the sun.

Every galaxy is a tension between being and nonbeing.

Those wide skies made me grateful to be alive and at one with their immensity. They let me feel the time as it passed, rather than constantly chase it as it seemed to rush away.

In the desert, nights were a spectacle and days came to an end more slowly.

I decided not to go back to New York after all.

Almost a quarter-century went by, and here in the desert I still am.

2

___

"I WAS HERE FIRST," we used to say, as kids.

We were there first: on the best play structure in the schoolyard, the one shaped like a rocket that could only hold one of us at a time. On the sofa at a party. In a good seat on the bus or at a sports event or in a movie theater: the one beside our friends.

The proclamation held weight with us. Not always—sometimes we'd choose to ignore it and go on to pick a fight—but often.

OK, we'd concede ruefully, bowing to the inevitable. You were here first. Respect.

Instinctively, on our fields of play, we were acting out an old idea: that firstness commanded deference.

Being somewhere first, among national powers and their colonial offshoots, has long established legal or common-law rights. In the US West, the doctrine of "prior appropriation" of water often governs the management of land, since land tenancy without access to water, in arid country, is useless. During pioneer days, when the expansionism of Manifest Destiny drove the federal government to offer free land to Caucasians occupying "new" territory, you could stake out a claim just by being white and setting foot in a place.

Across the globe, countries claim sovereignty over their land and waters based on firstness: they exist, and are acknowledged by the community of other nations, because they already existed. So they have enforceable borders, militaries, and other trappings of nation-statehood.

But the mighty among them have chosen to disregard that notion of first rights in the case of the native peoples whose lands they've occupied— first peoples they've killed off, enslaved, or displaced. To respect their own principle of firstness, when it comes to those groups, would be ethically right and politically absurd: voluntarily handing over property and power to those who have little of either.

As a conqueror species, we also disregard firstness.

It doesn't register with us that many creatures preexisted even our most distant ancestors and, over their extended and complicated history, directly shaped the spaces we now occupy. Most of us don't even know which of the other kinds are the true ancients and which, on the scale of evolutionary time, are as young as us.

Outside conservation biology circles, where native animals and plants are defended over exotic interlopers, the firstness of the beasts has little measurable effect on our behavior toward them. For the beasts, as for conquered peoples, history begins at the moment when the powerful consolidated their power.

Various species have endured for tens of millions of years—in some cases, more than 100 million or 200 million. Sea turtles, for instance. The birds, descended from dinosaurs. Their relatives the crocodilians. Ocean creatures like sponges and horseshoe crabs. The "primitive" fish known as sturgeon.

Club mosses, ginkgo trees, redwoods. Magnolias and palms.

Many of these now risk being wiped out within a single human lifetime.

Yet we're the guests in their house. Who came late to the party, set fire to the furniture, and gobbled up the hosts.

AT THE CENTER for Biological Diversity I work with activists. Scientists and lawyers, mostly, but also activists: they choose to be employed by a nonprofit, at much lower rates of pay than they could command in the for-profit sector, because they're drawn to the urgency of what they do. And I admire them. For their intelligence and skill, but also for their tenacity and the drudgery they endure—their willingness to perform endless iterations of the same task in defense of a disappearing world.

In my parallel life as a book writer, I work with editors and publicists and agents. I admire them also. Sometimes for similar reasons.

My presence in both of these subcultures is liminal—I float around on the margins. Neither fish nor fowl. Not really an activist, due to my aversion to slogans and crowds and open conflict. But also not a constant participant in the establishments of publishing or writing. Since the social and economic hub of publishing is New York, where I've chosen not to live. And since most literary writers also work as professors at universities, which I've chosen not to do.

ABOUT TWO DECADES AGO I got married to Kierán, who cofounded and still runs the Center. The email bulletins I'd first read, back in my New York grant-writing office, had come from his dusty and well-worn laptop. We were together nearly ten years—had children and, when the younger one had just turned three, got divorced.

He's a person whose mission comes first. But, like many mission-driven people, in an emergency he's at his best.

For a wedding present, a friend of his gave us a brief stay in her condo in the small Mexican seaside town of Puerto Peñasco, on the Gulf of California—Rocky Point, to Americans. This would be our honeymoon, and we would never take another.

Only an hour after we drove in, the trip was transformed into an ordeal when an explosion rocked a restaurant next to the one in which we were sitting. We'd just ordered margaritas, sitting on a terrace overlooking the ocean and some craggy rocks bleached white by seabird guano, when there was a roar of sound and a wave of pressure. The floor shook beneath our feet, and behind the bar rows of glasses and bottles shattered.

We got up, ran toward the source of the sound, and saw survivors fleeing

WE LOVED IT ALL 197

a burning building. Two elderly women seemed to be trapped on its rear, second-floor balcony, so Kierán climbed up and lifted them down to me.

I panicked as he did this, but he ignored me and went into the burning building. While I stood outside it.

He was an activist, even in that moment, and I was a bystander.

One of the women—she was in her nineties, a frail American traveler named Rose—had broken wrists and a deeply bruised chest.

Around us, as emergency vehicles began arriving and we looked for an ambulance to put Rose in, other victims wandered the street like zombies, in glassy-eyed shock. Several had odd-looking strips hanging from their arms.

I gazed at them and thought: Why do they all have those exact same ripped-up sleeves?

It took me a few moments to realize the ribbons weren't cloth but skin.

A faulty gas tank had exploded, and the town's bare-bones medical facilities weren't up to the task of triaging the many people who were badly injured—the ambulance we put Rose in was empty of medical equipment. It had no gurney. Or even a Band-Aid.

We spent the next two days translating between her and the doctor and scouring the town for a person she called "my young man Jerry," whom we eventually found in a separate medical facility. (For a while her description confounded our search, since Jerry proved to be in his late seventies.) We performed minor tasks for the couple, such as hunting through their burnt-out Jeep—of which only a ragged, black skeleton remained—for their passports and money so that Rose could be medevacked back to the States.

Though nothing was left of their other belongings, the documents and cash, in a melted hatch between the two front seats, were perfectly intact.

IN MY FAMILY of origin, politeness was valued more than argument, though we did debate lightly at the dinner table. We liked to interrupt each other in conversation and still do.

But conflict was avoided. Good manners, my parents explained when we failed to exhibit them, weren't arbitrary methods of control but a set of customs aimed at making others feel comfortable and at home.

Their faith was a faith in civility.

Kierán came from a quite different household: his parents were new immigrants to the United States when he was born. His English father, a civil engineer, left the family when Kierán was a boy. In the almost ten years we were together, I never met his father, though his wife sent Christmas gifts to our children.

But I did know his mother, a tiny woman whose large eyes were further magnified by her Coke-bottle glasses.

Maureen was a fervent Catholic from rural Ireland who'd grown up in a humble sod hut. She kept the bodily relics of ancestors she believed had been touched by the Holy Spirit and made pilgrimages to see manifestations of the image of the Virgin Mary.

On one visit she showed us a blurry black-and-white snapshot of a spot on her family farm in County Meath. In ballpoint pen on the photo, she'd drawn an *X* on an outside spot in front of a door—a threshold. The *X* marked the spot where her brother had, as she put it, dropped dead of a heart attack. The door had subsequently proved to be locked, on several occasions, *when no living person had locked it.* So her ballpoint *X* also signaled the location, from time to time, of his ghost.

My former mother-in-law believed in ghosts, but as a Catholic, not in divorce. Thus she refused to grant one to her absentee husband for years, even when he acquired a new family. Maureen was a nurse who worked long hours to keep her children in the good school district in which they'd been living when her husband left. So she was rarely home. Kierán and his two older siblings were often locked out of their house and left to roam the backyards and woods of their Cape Cod neighborhood with little supervision.

In modern parlance, with some positive spin, they were free-range kids.

When it came to right and wrong, Maureen was a conundrum. She considered herself pious and was observant of many Catholic rites.

But she submitted Kierán to surgery he didn't need, out of what we speculated might have been a case of Munchausen by proxy. And she also schooled him in shoplifting, which she lightheartedly called "nicking." She was always looking to game the system.

On the day of my wedding, she gave me something blue: a delicate silver pillbox topped in cobalt-colored enamel. I was surprised by the loveliness of the gift, since we shared, aesthetically, not so many tastes. She kept my writing vocation a secret from the rest of Kierán's extended family, for instance, due to the fact that my books were an embarrassment to her. They weren't, she said, about *successful* people like John Grisham's, which she preferred.

She bemoaned the fact that I wrote, instead, about unsuccessful and sometimes poor or pathetic people. Who, making matters worse, used swears. The four-letter words were printed right on the page—plain as the nose on your face.

I thanked her profusely for the keepsake. Got married.

And was later informed she'd nicked it from a dying patient.

Her older son is a successful venture capitalist, and after she visited one of his palatial homes she passed around photos from the trip to my own family, gathered in my far humbler house for Christmas. The pictures were not of people, as it turned out, but of her son's high-end kitchen appliances.

IN THEIR SEPARATE forms of physical and emotional abandonment Kierán's parents offered no models of steady parental care. But they did offer a repeated exposure to risk-taking and the violation of boundaries, which may have equipped him with a willingness to confront authority. And disrupt hierarchies.

Qualities that made him the activist he still is.

YOU NEED A measure of grandiosity, in ego and in visionary sweep, to struggle beyond the everyday. As well as a level of nutrition, wealth, and social support. So the movements and schools of thought that resist systemic injustice have often originated with the relatively privileged—a privilege, at least, of middle-classness. Karl Marx. Gandhi. Martin Luther King Jr. Greta Thunberg.

Yet on the progressive left, in the identity politics of the United States, privilege has become a marker of original sin. This tends to stymie progressives, since privilege also equates with mobility and access. Even the accusation of privilege foments damaging personality conflicts, on the left, as individuals vie to demonstrate their superior virtue in identity-based equity instead of engaging in the creative task conflicts that are needed to produce powerful results.

There are counterexamples, of course, to middle-classness as a prerequisite for revolutionary leadership: Frederick Douglass, say, who grew up a slave, so chilly in the night that he pulled a scavenged corn sack over his head for warmth. It was too short, so his legs stuck out of the bottom.

The cracks in his feet from long-term exposure to cold, he wrote, were so large he could rest a pen in them.

Young Douglass had books, though. One of them, which he carried everywhere, was called *The Columbian Orator*.

He immersed himself in language—political discourse, rhetoric, and history. And out of that language, created his own.

MUCH WRITING ABOUT climate change concerns itself with anxiety over the threat it poses to human property and institutions—as though property ownership and institutional power were not themselves the drivers of the crisis.

The author of one best-selling book about climate change issued a disclaimer, right up front, that he wasn't an environmentalist. Maybe he was simply being honest; maybe he wished to win over a mainstream readership by disavowing what he saw as a fringe; maybe "environmentalist" just has an unpleasant ring to it. And it's true that *environment* is a dry, technical-sounding word—the German version, *Umwelt*, is better, meaning "around-world."

WE LOVED IT ALL   201

He went on to mention that he was offended, on behalf of women and people of color, by recently raised notions of granting rights to non-human animals like primates and octopuses.

His angle seemed to be that said women and people of color, still newcomers to the hierarchy of the blessed, should feel demeaned and indignant at the suggestion that other categories of the living might also deserve consideration as subjects with rights.

Like schoolgirls, possibly, jealous of their friends' other friendships. Or wives demanding that their husbands shield their eyes from the attractiveness of strange women who pass them on the street.

To him the suggestion of broadening the scope of our empathy insulted those women and minorities by equating them with the beasts.

But no one had equated anyone with the beasts. Except, implicitly, the author himself.

In fact many of the scientists doing the most groundbreaking work on the sentience and subjectivity of animals, and now plants, are women—have been since the early primate research of Jane Goodall and Dian Fossey and Biruté Mary Galdikas. On chimps, gorillas, and orangutans, respectively.

And numerous cultures and groups outside the European diaspora live far closer to an animistic worldview than humanist critics in New York.

3

—

ORANGUTAN MEANS "PERSON OF THE FOREST" in Malay. The only great apes in Asia, they're also the least aggressive and most solitary of primates. One of their three species was only first described in 2017.

Males have face pads called flanges along each cheek, like puffy jowls that get bigger as they age; females prefer males with large flanges. "Flanged" males.

A few Bornean orangutans who've lived among people have adopted human behaviors and playthings. One sits beside David Attenborough in an episode of *BBC Earth* carefully scrubbing at fabric with soap. Another uses a hammer on a nail and saws a board. A third travels down the river in a canoe with a baby sitting on her lap, steering and paddling with her hands.

Numerous zookeepers have reported on orangutans' apparent ability to understand human intentions and speech even when they haven't been taught any words. Some of these captives like to draw and game using tablets; since their grip is too powerful for the delicate devices, the computers are held by keepers or attached to the outsides of their enclosures, with images projected inside.

One who lived in the Omaha Zoo in the 1960s, called Fu Manchu, was so good at picking the lock of his enclosure with a homemade wire key—which he kept hidden in his mouth—that he was made an honorary member of the American Association of Locksmiths. He'd open his enclosure at night and let out the other orangutans, but they wouldn't go far: all would be found in the morning, resting in the surrounding trees.

Sumatra's Tapanuli orangutans are the rarest great apes of all: around eight hundred are thought to exist in the wild. They live only in trees and have not yet been observed climbing down to the ground— possibly they hesitate because they share their three small forest patches with a remnant population of tigers. But the tigers are a lesser danger. It's a hydroelectric plant and dam, for which the orangutans' forest was already being cleared by Chinese companies in 2018, that threaten to drive them extinct.

At the Barcelona Zoo, where my friend Jenny and I went to visit Snowflake the famous albino gorilla in the 1990s, we saw Snowflake looking miserable and alone in a small cage. With cigarette butts being dropped and ground out at his feet. We were already sad when we walked on to the orangutan exhibit, where men were jeering and hurling balled-up garbage at the orangutans. Hard. And cackling loudly when the projectiles hit their marks.

The orangutans made no move to defend themselves. No snarls, no teeth-baring.

They sat without moving, enduring the barrage.

Already confined to a small space with nowhere to hide, the gentle apes were being punished for an uncommitted crime.

They were young men, the garbage-throwers. In the age range of most mass shooters, serial killers, and drunk drivers. There were many of them, and we were only two women. They were at home, and we were tourists.

So we too failed to move.

SHAME IS A curious sensation. Like guilt, it tells you what you should have done. But more. Where guilt has a mechanical aspect— feels like a nod of the mind to moral error—shame permeates the spirit. It seems to show you not only what you should have done, but who you should have been.

Who you should always be.

TO COMBAT THE advance of the climate-change juggernaut, the best-selling writer suggested, we should embrace our notion of human exceptionalism as a duty and responsibility rather than flee from it: the "anthropic principle," as he put it.

And there's nothing wrong with taking ownership of the predicament we're in—we need to do so speedily. That author's view of human exceptionalism is a standard one, implicit in many of our assumptions about the human race as separate, chosen, and better or higher than other forms of life.

Still, "exceptionalism," an assertion of the superiority of one group or individual over others, is identical to supremacy—the same impulse with a politer name. We award it to our species as though doing so were the basic truth and a morally neutral act.

After all, the rest of the living, who exist outside the realm of our language, can hardly rise up in outrage to defend themselves.

And the history of white and male supremacy is also the history of human supremacy. Over the past few centuries, white domination of the socioeconomic world has been solidified on a global scale along with the runaway exploitation of the natural world, and most of the benefits from that subjugation and liquidation have flowed to white people. And been largely controlled by white males.

White and human supremacy, and the domination of women by men, are so entangled that the mental project of separating them requires a torturous logic.

So I couldn't help hearing echoes, in the author's invocation of our duty to embrace our "exceptional" status and save the world for the benefit of our own kind, of Rudyard Kipling's poem "The White Man's Burden."

In which the chosen, ascendant leaders of the kingdom of God on earth are enjoined to take control of those of a lower, browner order—in the case of Kipling's poem, the citizens of the Philippines—who are their "new-caught sullen peoples / Half devil and half child."

For the glory of empire.

EMPIRE IS MOST glorious by far when set to music. Stirring national anthems for the general population, marching songs for the soldiers, soaring hymns for the congregations. Nostalgic barracks lullabies like "Lili Marlene."

But everything is glorious. Set to music.

AT AN ELEPHANT SANCTUARY in Thailand where most of the elephants are former logging-industry workers, a British musician named Paul Barton serenades them by playing the piano. Bach, Chopin, and Beethoven. I've seen these performances on YouTube.

The elephants—some blind, some scarred, some merely elderly—stand patiently, swaying slightly to the music, flicking their tails and flapping their ears. One or two mischievous individuals try to join in the playing, or possibly distract the pianist, by hitting the keys repeatedly with their trunks.

Most remain quiet and motionless. Listening.

ASIAN ELEPHANTS HAVE been working animals for millennia, transporting people and goods through forests that have no roads, harvesting lumber from those forests, and conducting daring rescues across rushing rivers in the monsoon season.

The logging elephants are trained by mahouts, their drivers and constant companions, to execute complicated maneuvers with timber—

manipulations that require advance visualization and at times reflect an understanding of geometry and mechanics that many people don't possess, myself among them. These elephants' relationships with the mahouts are close but bound by literal chains and sometimes painful master-slave dynamics.

As the geographer Jacob Shell documented in his book *Giants of the Monsoon Forest*, logging elephants in Burma usually begin their lives living wild. They're captured using a brutal chase-and-lasso strategy known as *mela shikar* during which they're ripped away from their families. And from then on compelled to lead lives of servitude.

At night, when the elephants' work is done, they're allowed to roam through the forest near the encampments. Not free—since they wear chains and bells so that they can be easily found in the morning—but not tied down. There they can eat, so the mahouts don't have to feed them, and sometimes mate with still-wild elephants before returning to work the next day.

Shell has taken the ethically complicated step of advocating for the persistence of this system of forced elephant labor on the basis that their "partnership" with people in the timber industry may be their best shot at survival. Deforestation, rather than hunting, is the main threat to the survival of Asian elephants, and logging by elephant is less destructive to those forests than mechanized methods.

Alternate models for protecting elephants, like preserves, have not proved viable in the region and show little potential for doing so in the near future.

Shell supports the continued enslavement of these elephants—for now—as a conservation strategy.

Even slavery, he writes, is preferable to extinction.

4

—

IN SEVENTEENTH-CENTURY QUEBEC, Catholics were forbidden to eat red meat on Fridays; some still observe this prohibition. But the local beavers' meat, which was abundant and came in a dark, rich shade of red, proved delicious.

And after all, along with their tree-felling and river-engineering prowess, the beavers were excellent swimmers.

So the church decreed that, under its law, they were fish.

LAW IS AN obvious instrument of language—its literal deployment as an embodiment of social will. It should be a shield but is also a weapon.

In 2010 a landmark decision was handed down by the US Supreme Court on a political-campaign finance case ironically known as *Citizens United*. In it the high court ruled 5–4 that corporations had the free speech rights of persons. Under the Constitution, it said, corporations *were* persons. And like persons, they had a right to speak.

The sly alchemy of the court's reasoning enabled it to claim that companies are people because they're made up of groups of them—despite the fact that companies don't otherwise function as persons, under the law, due to the presence of relief valves like limited liability. They don't have the responsibilities of persons and are awarded privileges regular people don't have, such as not paying federal income tax, purely by incorporating.

Not only that, but the person-corporations' words *were the same as their money*, said the court.

Since corporate words are protected under the First Amendment, so is the right to spend unlimited corporate money on political campaigns.

By means of the *Citizens United* decision, one person, one vote became barely even a technical truth. Companies that had deep pockets but represented the interests of a minuscule, wealthy group could now substantially decide who won elections and, to a greater extent than ever before, what policies got made.

Supreme Court Justice John Paul Stevens, then eighty-nine years old and faltering, wrote a ninety-page dissent to the majority opinion and read aloud from it—albeit with great difficulty—for twenty minutes.

The president at the time, Barack Obama, was a centrist and a constitutional lawyer. He respected the independence of the judiciary and rarely offered up personal views on Supreme Court decisions. But after the ruling on *Citizens United*, even this careful and moderate politician felt compelled to speak out.

"I can't think of anything more devastating to the public interest," he said.

THE BESTOWING OF any measure of civil rights on nonhuman animals is a high bar, particularly under a judicial regime bent on narrowing the definition of basic human rights rather than expanding it. As it stands now, even preventing the extreme suffering of complex sentient creatures in lab settings is a byzantine legal struggle.

Katherine Meyer, a Harvard law professor I've met who's fought for kindness toward other animals for most of her career, submitted a petition—along with a number of other lawyers, scientists, and scholars—to the National Institutes of Health in the summer of 2020.

It requested that, based on their intelligence and sensitivity, cephalopods like octopuses and cuttlefish be granted animal status.

Science clearly defines invertebrates as animals. To propose that an octopus is not an animal is as rational as claiming that beavers are fish.

But only warm-blooded animals are covered by the Animal Welfare Act (minus the ones used most in research—rats, mice, and birds—and of course livestock). And only those organisms legally defined as animals have any protection from cruel mistreatment.

The granting of personhood to lifeforms beyond the human, who can feel pain, produce young, eat and sleep, and like people are born and die, remains out of the question.

But personhood *isn't* only for people, in the United States.

For the awarding of personhood to corporate entities that do not feel pain—and which we don't hold responsible for criminal acts, as we do people, except for slap-on-the-wrist fines when their executives get caught—is a done deal.

IN THIS COUNTRY it's mostly state law that deals with the matter of cruelty to other animals. Like the education of children, it's seen as a game with stakes that aren't crucial to national welfare.

As a result, the playing field and the sponsorship of teams are left to the little guys.

Three major federal laws touch on the subject. The Endangered Species Act protects endangered animals held in captivity, as well as those living wild, from what it calls "take"—harassment, harm, and killing. And then there are the Humane Slaughter Act and the Animal Welfare Act, on the books since 1958 and 1966.

The law about animal slaughter essentially says you can't torture animals meant for eating. You have to kill them before, not after, you shackle them, hoist them, or cut them up.

It excludes all poultry, despite the fact that birds make up nine out of ten US animals killed for food every year.

The Animal Welfare Act, catalyzed by citizens' reports of their pet cats and dogs being kidnapped for lab experiments, requires the US Department of Agriculture to set standards for the humane handling of certain animals that *aren't* livestock—those being used in research, for exhibition and entertainment, and in the pet trade. Researchers, exhibitors, and dealers are prohibited from violating those standards.

Since no cold-blooded animals are protected by the law, reptiles, fish, amphibians, and all invertebrates are excluded, and mice and rats are specifically exempt.

In 2010 a fourth federal law dealing with animal cruelty was passed, with a smaller purview: it prohibited the distribution of "crush" videos that were circulating on the internet. Footage of women's feet, for example, in high-heeled shoes, stomping repeatedly on kittens.

This Obama-era law did not prohibit the acts themselves.

IN 2019, IN THE midst of a corruption scandal and impeachment inquiry that dominated the screens, President Donald Trump signed the PACT Act, which went further than the Obama law on torture videos by criminalizing the acts of "crushing, burning, drowning, suffocating, impaling, and other bodily injury toward any nonhuman mammals, birds, reptiles, or amphibians."

He announced the revised statute the same day he trotted out a hero dog for the cameras—a military K-9 from a raid that had just ended with an Islamic State terrorist blowing himself up (along with three of his children). A triumphant victory, the president crowed. Expressed no regret, even in passing, about the three dead kids.

"He died like a dog," he said, with characteristic tone deafness, of Abu Bakr al-Baghdadi.

While celebrating an actual dog with fanfare.

That dog—named after the talk show host Conan O'Brien—was subsequently put out to stud to dog owners in pro-Trump states, according to one report. They were charged a fee of $10,000 per penetration, with the profits going to the president's personal legal defense fund.

The law's passage—notable for the inclusion of some cold-blooded animals as a protected class—went largely unnoticed.

5

—

WHAT DO THE others know that we never will? What do they see, hear, and feel that we never have?

What forms of the extraordinary lie in their ordinary natures?

IN HIS BOOK *The Hidden Life of Trees*, Peter Wohlleben, a German forest manager, became famous and controversial for writing about trees as beings with agency. Drawing on the work of scientists and his own observations, Wohlleben discussed healthy forests as sentient communities in which trees have freedom, cohesion, a capacity for family life, and even intelligence.

Trees living outside such communities, he suggested—in plots of dirt surrounded by pavement on city sidewalks, say, or single-species, single-age stands grown in rows to be cut down for lumber or Christmas—exist in a lonely captivity.

Apart from others of their species and unable to communicate or reproduce, he argued, trees outside forests are much like zoo or lab animals.

His description of their isolation reminds me of the phrase *death in life*, used by the psychiatrist and author Robert Jay Lifton as the title of his book on the *hibakusha*—those Japanese people who survived the US dropping of atomic bombs on Hiroshima and Nagasaki.

While I was researching a novel about the physicists of the Manhattan Project, I went to those cities and met two *hibakusha*. Conversed with them through an interpreter.

Both were elderly—this was the early 2000s—and must have been asked the same questions countless times. By Americans like me, self-interested emissaries from the land of the old enemy. Come to investigate. Come to spectate. Or make a reckoning.

What was it like. What do you remember. What do you want people to know.

But they were flawlessly patient, exhibiting a gentle forbearance.

Many *hibakusha* lived on into the twenty-first century. At first, resoundingly alone.

In the aftermath of a split second that had robbed them of every person they had ever known or loved.

I WANTED TO learn firsthand, when I was writing my novel about the men who developed nuclear weapons, not only about them but about the cities where the atomic bombs had been dropped. And the people who had lived there then.

I knew my research would be amateurish—I'm neither a journalist nor a historian—but I also knew I had to go. A personal pilgrimage, I guess.

I'd already traveled to the Trinity Site, in the white sands of New Mexico, where the first bomb was dropped from a rickety tower in the desert. And where Oppenheimer pronounced the famous line from the Bhagavad Gita, *I am become Death, the destroyer of worlds.* I'd followed a tour group of nuclear regulators, disgorged from a bus, wearing laminated government badges and carrying brown-bag lunches. They sat on rocks and ate their sandwiches, gazing at the orange wildflowers growing near ground zero.

I'd traveled to the Nevada Test Site, to radioactive dumps, to a Titan missile silo south of Tucson, to Santa Fe and Los Alamos. I couldn't finish the book without going to Japan as well.

In Hiroshima, after I interviewed the *hibakusha*, we saw a Peace Clock that resets to zero every time a bomb is tested—an echo of the Doomsday Clock, that rare, enduring act of performance art by scientists that shows how close we are, at any given moment, to midnight.

It now reflects not only the threat of nuclear war, but of climate change; when we visited Hiroshima it was set at seven minutes to midnight. Just after I began to write this book it ticked the closest it had ever been, one hundred seconds to midnight. Where it remains.

We wandered through gardens of pink azaleas and looked at monuments. The Peace Memorial. The Monument of the Atomic Bomb Sacrifice. The Children's Peace Monument, where all the dead children are represented by the figure of Sadako Sasaki, a girl who was two when the bomb was dropped and lived on to be twelve, folding a thousand cranes as she slowly died of radiation sickness.

We were atomic tourists. Feeling the mingling of horror and helplessness that such a position brings.

A CANADIAN ECOLOGIST named Suzanne Simard, who was raised in a timber-industry family and for a while worked in the industry herself, now studies the communal life of trees—their sharing of food among species, their caretaking of their young, and their communication. Which occurs through networks of mycorrhizal fungi, among other means. Her work has shown that older trees are often hubs of these communities and that they cooperate by sharing nutrients and carbon, sometimes sacrificing themselves for their offspring. And that trees can even warn each other of some kinds of environmental change.

And Monica Gagliano, an Italian Australian marine ecologist turned plant scientist, believes she's discovering evidence, through experiments on plants like mimosas and peas, of their ability to anticipate and learn. Potted mimosas called "shameplants," whose leaves fold inward when they're threatened, were dropped six inches through the air repeatedly, but onto a cushion so that the drop did no harm. Over time they learned when *not* to fold inward—retaining, for nearly a month, that memory of safety.

Her findings call into question, among other assumptions, the distinctions of being and ethics that we make around the terms *animal* and *plant*.

Both Gagliano and Simard deliberately use "anthropomorphic" language to describe the behavior of the organisms of the green world.

Gagliano doesn't claim to know how plants achieve their memory. But her experiments on their responses to events, patterned on Pavlov's famous studies of dogs, appear to be repeatable.

It's the language she uses to describe her conclusions—applying the words *learning* and *cognition* to green organisms, for instance—that draws indignation from the biology community. Its reactions to her use of such terminology have been so defensive it's clear that many mainstream biologists see her words as a threat.

To the more orthodox among them, her suggestion that plants, like other living beings, may possess subjecthood is a scientific heresy.

THE RED-BROWN HAWKS that visit my garden hunt in families, which is unusual for birds of prey: their feeding strategies more closely resemble wolves'.

Like eagles and other raptors, these Harris's hawks can see in minute resolution for miles, at a distance four to eight times greater than people. They see both farther and faster than we do.

But Harris's hawks see more slowly than, say, falcons. Scientists who've studied the high "temporal resolution" of raptor vision believe this is because the small mammals they eat move over the ground. While falcons need to see faster to hunt the prey they seek, which is other birds.

Like all birds active in daytime, hawks perceive more colors than we do, too. Their eyes have four color cones instead of our three and are sensitive to ultraviolet light, which our eyes can't detect.

Birds see an array of colors that, according to evolutionary biologist Mary Stoddard, who studies UV vision in hummingbirds, "humans cannot even imagine."

Native only to the Americas, hummingbirds count among their number the world's smallest bird species—the bee hummingbird of Cuba, about two inches long. Among birds they have the largest brains, relative to their bodies.

Those brains are still tiny, but they feature multidirectional sensing that helps hummingbirds to hover in midair, rotating their wings in a figure-eight motion.

The birds' encyclopedic memories allow them to return to the same flowers, in the same gardens, during their solitary annual migrations of thousands of miles.

One study conducted on rufous hummingbirds in 2013 suggests that, like us, they have access to what's called episodic memory, storing "*what, where* and *when* as separate pieces of information, as is thought to be the case for human episodic memory."

THE LEAFCUTTER ANTS who live in my garden can strip a bush of all its leaves and flowers in a single night. I've stepped out my door in the morning and seen yesterday's lush, green bush turned into a bundle of stems.

The bushes usually recover. But the speed of the ants' defoliation is shocking and impressive.

They leave thick, bright trails of the leaves or flowers they're moving weaving across the sand and rocks. The trails are sometimes green, sometimes yellow, sometimes purple or white. After carting the plant material back to their underground nests, they ferment it in masses of fungus the colony can eat. They're one of only a handful of animals on earth who practice the cultivation of their own food.

The cultures of ants are diverse. Amazonian worker ants in the genus *Polyergus* appear to conduct slavery on a grand scale, utterly reliant on it for their survival. For *Polyergus* workers have developed without the ability to care for the brood or even feed themselves. In well-orchestrated raids, they kidnap *Formica* ants from their home colonies and take the pupae back to the hive, where they're raised by previously captured *Formica*, now adults.

The younger kidnapped ants then go to work for their new masters.

This, anyway, is how we frame their behavior. Whether the slave ants experience their lives as a painful bondage or a form of community service—or neither—we have no idea.

PRAIRIE DOGS HAVE been poisoned, in their grassland homes, for over a century by government agencies at the behest of livestock owners. As prey they're key to the diet of black-footed ferrets, which were also nearly taken out, in a domino effect, by prairie-dog eradication campaigns.

The researcher Con Slobodchikoff, who's studied prairie dog communication for more than three decades, believes their calls are so sophisticated and complex that they qualify as language. These calls convey, he says, not only the type of predator but its shape, size, color, and speed—and can even be modified to describe creatures the prairie dogs haven't seen before.

Slobodchikoff and his colleagues conducted an experiment in which they walked through prairie dog colonies garbed in a range of colored shirts. When they wore white lab coats, the calls were similar (except when the prairie dogs spotted "one especially short researcher").

But for each nonwhite color the biologists wore, the prairie dogs made different calls.

SOMEWHERE ALONG THE WAY, in the past couple of years—without meaning to—I seem to have simplified the falling-asleep imagery that used to be so labor-intensive for me.

These days, instead of picturing myself on the back of a bird when I feel exhausted but sleepless, I picture myself *as* the bird.

No longer a passenger, I imagine myself inside a bird's streamlined and hollow-boned body. Glide along on a current of air, knowing only the rhythmic up-and-down movement of my wings.

I can nearly sense how the wings, on their downstroke, lift me up.

And then, as I raise them, allow me to sink again.

Projecting myself into the body of another, I feel weightless.

HUMAN EYES ARE distinctive for the white sclera surrounding our irises that makes it easy for other people to see where we're looking. In 2001 Tokyo researchers published a paper showing that we have the largest white-to-pupil ratio of any primate—along with unusually horizontally elongated eye shapes that allow this white part, and its contrasting dark iris and pupil, to be well displayed.

They put forth a "cooperative eye hypothesis," suggesting our large sclerae evolved to allow us faster communication of intention and attention within groups.

Being able to perceive the direction of each other's gazes, they propose, gave us an advantage in the collaborative social behavior that has allowed us to build massive societies.

The big eyes of purple octopuses make them look like cartoons. Those eyes remind me of people's—you can make out a ring of white around the dark center.

IT'S DIFFICULT TO overstate the exceptional qualities of an octopus. These playful tool-users can mimic different undersea organisms, not merely in an act of blending into their immediate surroundings, but by taking on their colors and shapes when the organisms being mimicked aren't present. With almost no hard parts inside them, they're accomplished escape artists that can move their entire, sometimes substantial bodies through holes that seem impossibly small.

They have distinct personalities and are probably the most intelligent of all invertebrates. As the philosopher and diver Peter Godfrey-Smith puts it—he's devoted much time and thought to octopuses and cuttlefish—they may be nature's sole experiment, among boneless creatures, with a large brain.

Craig Foster, a South African filmmaker who recorded his relationship with a single octopus by visiting her kelp-forest den every day for a year, was enraptured by the animal's intelligence. In the resulting film *My Octopus Teacher* he shows how she surrounded herself entirely in hastily picked-up clamshells to evade a shark predator. (A similar shark had previously bitten off one of her arms, which regrew afterward into a perfect new one.) Covered in the shimmering shells, she looked nothing like an octopus to me.

But the shark, operating on scent, was not fooled and grabbed the shell-bedecked octopus in his jaws.

At that point Foster had to swim up to the surface to breathe—his filming was done while free-diving, without a scuba tank—and when he dove down again, she'd somehow maneuvered her way, still covered in shells, onto the shark's back.

Where his teeth could not reach her.

Finally, when the predator swam beneath an overhanging shelf of reef and vegetation, she released her hold on his back and dropped all the shells in an instant, slipping into a crevice and saving herself.

Effectively octopuses have nine brains, depending on how you define them, including one in each arm. They can unscrew the childproof caps on medicine bottles and figure out how to short-circuit lights.

They have sharp memories and, like crows, can recognize individual people—as prairie dogs do—even if those people are wearing identical uniforms.

PEOPLE IN SEARCH OF mental or emotional relief are encouraged to "live in the present." The act of present dwelling, when we can achieve it, promises mindfulness and tranquility. Various high-end spas around Tucson sell mindfulness at a premium—for a thousand dollars a night you can learn to be mindful, get your nails done, and also eat fine food.

But mindfulness, whether premium or not, is a genuine skill. It's a respite from storytelling: to the extent that we're able, for a sustained moment in experience, to extricate ourselves from the ongoing narrative of past and future that orders our lives, we have a chance to feel untethered. To be suspended beyond the constant process of interpretation, decision, and meaning-making that harries our neural pathways. Simply absorb the presence of the world and our presence within it.

Maybe this present dwelling is a gift for an octopus as well. Possibly these sensitive and ingenious animals, who can't pass down their experience or stories to their children, exist in a liquid of time as well as space. That allows them to live lightly in the dance of fluid beauty their morphic bodies convey.

Or maybe, for an octopus, the cycle of life is more like the curse of Sisyphus, doomed always to push a boulder up, up, up a hill, in the depths of Hades to which Zeus had exiled him. Only to have it roll back down again.

Maybe it's both.

6

BEFORE I GOT MARRIED, in Tucson, I'd been single for a while when I met a guy in a downtown bar. He was a mortgage lender then, though he didn't enjoy the job, and worked for a company that would soon be implicated in a housing crisis caused by lenders like him selling mortgages to people who couldn't afford them.

And subsequently, in large numbers, lost their homes.

We didn't have much in common, but we stayed together for a year and a half anyway, mostly due to my refusal to recognize the mismatch. In the end he broke up with me in a curt long-distance phone call.

He'd always said I was judgmental—a claim that was hard to refute, since I certainly enjoy the formulation of opinions. And have for most of my life.

One of the judgments that most annoyed him concerned a motivational-speaking outfit to which he was committed. It was the updated version of a seventies organization called EST, known then as Landmark Education. Or more casually "the Forum."

Landmark is a private corporation that offers services in "personal development" to individuals and businesses. Occasional efforts to label it a cult have been met with defamation lawsuits or the threat thereof. Whenever my boyfriend brought it up in conversation I'd roll my eyes, and he'd say, with some bitterness, that I didn't know what I was talking about.

That was factually accurate. And so, despite a vague worry about being sucked into a cult, I decided to sign up for a course.

It was a two-day deal held in a bland hotel conference room in Phoenix. Fluorescent lighting brought everyone's pores and personal-grooming missteps into harsh relief—I fixated unpleasantly on the dandruff sprinkled across the shoulders of a guy sitting in front of me. *Judgment. Judgment. Judgment.* And the nervous mastication of a woman to my right, who kept unwrapping pieces of gum. She folded so many sticks into her mouth in a row that I had to conclude she was swallowing them like candy. You weren't allowed to eat during the sessions, so maybe the gum was her work-around.

A man lectured from behind a podium, which I appreciated, and then asked the audience to perform "encounter" tasks, which I did not. The one that made me cringe most was an exercise in which we were told to write on our name tags "I am the possibility of . . ." and then fill in the blank.

Next we were asked to circulate within the whitely lit room—without the benefit of even the most meager cocktail—and meet our fellow personality developers. Participants milled around with labels on their chests that said things like: *I am the possibility of . . . unconditional love. I am the possibility of . . . emotional bravery. I am the possibility of . . . speaking Truth to Power.*

I wasn't aiming so high. My name tag said *I am the possibility of . . . good conversation.*

In that moment, however, I wasn't embracing even that modest potential.

Still, as far as I could tell, the company didn't have the hallmarks of a cult: no one tried to separate you from your family, induce you to sign over the deed to your condo, or force you to subsume your identity into that of a charismatic leader. Maybe there *were* some charismatic leaders, but the ones I met seemed more like sports coaches or driving instructors.

And as it turned out, the substance of the patter was solid. It seemed to have been gleaned—though its sources weren't credited—from philosophers like Heidegger: We all have our lives, said the language "technology," as the company called it. We have our lives and the stories we tell about our lives. Those two are not the same.

When the Forum leader hammered home this distinction in his lecture, I felt genuinely pleased that the corporation was bringing philosophy into the personal-development sphere.

If more of us recognized the stories we told about ourselves—their biases and contradictions and how often, though we steer ourselves by their landmarks, they diverge from our lived experience—how much freer might we be? How much more self-aware?

I went back to my boyfriend and told him I'd been wrong. I wouldn't go back to the Forum, myself, I said. A little goes a long way. But I had to admit he'd been right: there *was* merit in what the company offered.

He smiled and said, But it's not about being right.

I said, It's not?

He said, The need to be right is part of the story you tell yourself about your life.

I said, Sure, yeah, OK. But then, what *is* it about, actually?

He said, It's about being open to possibility.

STORYTELLING WILL NEVER be the same as action. But action depends on a perception of possibility, which only arises from the tales we tell ourselves.

AN ORANGUTAN NAMED Sandra is the single beast, so far, who's ever been given personhood-type rights by a court of law. She lived in a zoo in Buenos Aires that had become notorious for its poor treatment of its wards, and her case was taken to court by animal rights advocates. In 2015 she was recognized as a "nonhuman person" by a judge in Argentina and given the right to life, liberty, and freedom from suffering.

The decision was reversed on appeal, since the category "nonhuman person" does not exist in the Argentine Civil Code.

But Sandra still had her liberty. Since there are no refuges for apes in Argentina, she waited for almost five years for travel permits. In 2019 she was taken to a sanctuary in Florida, where she lives with other orangutans and chimpanzees, some of whom were once pop-culture celebrities.

Bubbles, the chimpanzee who used to belong to Michael Jackson. Ripley, who appeared on *Seinfeld*. Along with other chimpanzee and orangutan actors whose working lives were over. Butch, a circus chimp at Ringling Bros. who'd been castrated and had most of his teeth removed, passed through a biomedical facility and a roadside zoo before reaching the sanctuary.

In 2020, during the COVID pandemic, an Asian elephant named Mara was also moved from that defunct Argentine zoo. Beginning in the 1970s, before she came to the zoo, Mara had been a circus performer—a role she apparently didn't take to, for once, like Topsy, she killed a trainer.

Unlike Topsy, though, she wasn't executed for her crime. After decades of living in her small enclosure with two African elephants whose company she didn't appreciate, she was taken to a refuge in Brazil.

The 1,700-mile journey was arduous for elephant and handlers alike—the *New York Times* ran a feature documenting the odyssey—but when it was over she "quickly bonded" with another Asian elephant at the refuge.

And was left there to live out the rest of her life beneath the trees.

WILD PLACES ARE also being contemplated, on rare occasions, as candidates for the legal status of personhood. On the lands occupied by the United States, such place-personhood has only, as I write this, been granted by a tribal government: that of the Yurok, which in 2019 gave legal personhood status to the Klamath River in California.

Although such gestures have so far been marginal and frankly unthreatening to the status quo, countermeasures to block them are already being

taken. In Idaho, in February 2022, a Republican state legislator introduced a bill to ban all efforts to grant any personhood to nature.

In New Zealand two places have been given the status of persons: a
rainforest called Te Urewera and a river called the Whanganui. There the
Maori tribes known as the Tuhoe and the Whanganui are the appointed
guardians of, respectively, the forest and the river.

IN DR. SEUSS'S picture book *The Lorax*, my early-childhood favorite,
a factory that makes clothes out of trees has destroyed the forest, along
with its birds and fishes and bears. A landscape bright with color and life
and the sounds of animals has turned brown and dead.

This story will repeat itself, the narrator warns a child.

Unless.

This narrator is the Once-ler, concealed in his derelict tower—save for
two eyes we can see through a window and a long, green, wrinkled pair of
arms that extend out of it—who tells his tale to a little boy.

In exchange for fifteen cents, a nail, and the shell of a great-
great-great-grandfather snail.

Like the children reading his story, the little boy doesn't care what
the Once-ler looks like. He barely cares who's talking to him, much as
elementary school students show minimal interest in the qualifications or
lives of their teachers.

Picture books for kids rarely contain author photos. Whereas, in
books written for adults, such photos are mandatory. Adult readers
demand to be presented with a picture of the storyteller—even as far
back as the seventeenth century, a friend with expertise in the history of
books tells me, it was important to present an engraved image of a book's
author as a frontispiece.

For Dr. Seuss's little boy, the storyteller's identity and selfhood aren't
the point. What matters is the story the hermit has to tell.

As it turns out, the Once-ler was once a young man who built a factory that destroyed the place the boy would later live in. While a scolding

creature called the Lorax—a proxy for both environmentalists and the beasts whose interests they try to represent—issued him constant warnings that he never heeded.

Part of the perfect conceit of the book is its nearly invisible protagonist. Not the boy, who's a framing device. And not the Lorax, its conscience, who would simply have said "I told you so" and come off preachy.

Rather it's the world-weary villain. Making his confession.

Grown wise and sad in the wake of a trail of desolation.

NONE OF US wishes to extend a wrinkled arm from a boarded-up shack, down the road, then pull up a bucket of garbage and say to a kid: If only you could have seen it, the way it used to be.

How glorious it was, before you were around!

How marvelous they were, the creatures who once lived with us here.

7

JOURNALISTIC ACCOUNTS, SCIENTIFIC reports written for lay readers, and sometimes even books and movies tell nonfictional or semi-fictional stories of individual animals' biographies.

These include popular films like *Free Willy*, based on the "true story" of Keiko the killer whale, or orca, who played him in the movie. Orcas have come to be called killer whales because they're killers *of* whales—among other prey—but in fact they're in the dolphin family.

Our babysitter Pat showed my son *Free Willy* many times when he was little. Sy made an exception to his usual ban on watching live-action animal movies for Pat's sake, even though he knew he'd have to endure her tears of empathetic joy when Willy was finally freed.

Outside pure fiction, the animals' subjectivity and interior experience don't need to be constructed; their behavior can simply be shown, their lives observed and interpreted. Chiefly by the ways those lives intersect with the lives of individual humans.

But as with people, this rarely translates to telling the stories of the animal multitudes.

Or the multitudes' decline.

Once collectivity is mentioned, we begin to yawn.

ORCA FEMALES, LIKE human ones, go on living for decades after they lose the ability to reproduce. Orcas are matriarchal, and the grandmothers play a crucial role in raising the next generations: males are known to die younger in their absence. Their brains are huge, and the limbic lobes of those brains—associated, in people, with emotional life and the formation of memories—are larger, relative to their size, and more complex than our own.

Their pods communicate in different dialects, with distinct "signature calls" for different individuals. Names, in other words.

The members of one group, the fish-eating orcas who live around Puget Sound and are referred to as "Southern Residents," have been given names by people, too. Their population was hit hard by a spree of captures for aquariums in the 1960s and '70s—more than 250 killer whales were taken from their homes back then, over a ten-year period, from that population and others. Like Keiko, the first captive orca to be rereleased into the wild.

By 2023 only 73 Southern Residents remained.

One mother orca, known to biologists as J35 and the media as Tahlequah, was captured on video in 2018 mourning her dead calf. The baby had died soon after it was born—not unusual in recent history, since the salmon that Southern Residents depend on have grown scarce, mostly due to dams and water diversions and human fishing, and the whales are slowly starving.

Along with other female orcas, the grieving mother was seen engaged in some kind of "ritual," as a watcher said, immediately after the death. Six or seven whales surrounded the baby's body in a close circle and kept it under a moving beam of moonlight.

Then, for seventeen days and a thousand miles, Tahlequah pushed her baby's body through the water till she let it go.

AMONG BALEEN WHALES, who strain food through their sieve-like mouths as they swim rather than lunging and biting it as orcas do, blue whales are king: the largest animals ever to have lived on earth. They were once abundant across the global ocean. Within the span of a century, about 99 percent were killed off by hunting—some 350,000, by one estimate.

This was the period that followed the invention of the explosive harpoon, in 1844, and ended in the mid-1960s, when commercial whaling of the species was outlawed.

Most populations have been slowly rebounding, and some 5,000 to 15,000 mature blue whales are thought to be alive now. But the study of their lives and anatomies is made difficult by the fact that—unless struck and killed by a ship or, more rarely, tangled up in a fishing net and washed ashore—they sink to the bottom of the sea after they die.

Whale fall, we say.

In shallow waters, with sunlight and heat and an abundance of carrion-eaters, their bodies disappear quickly. But at great depths the process can last for decades.

Whale fall occurs when a whale body comes to rest in the pelagic bathyal or abyssal zones—the latter stretching down as far as 20,000 feet. A place of perpetual darkness.

On the bottom of the deep ocean, under a faint, dreamlike drift of "marine snow" made up of particles of organic material that slowly sink toward the seafloor, their great bodies turn into gardens. Banquets for deep-sea fish and crustaceans and other passersby who are hungry. Purple octopuses settle on the carcass to eat its scavengers, and bone-eating worms secrete an acid that dissolves the whales' huge skeletons.

Submersibles have captured footage of the immovable feast. So we know a little about the afterlives of blue whales, but not much at all about the lives themselves.

The peaceful leviathans are still a mystery.

THE US NAVY has trained dolphins and other marine mammals since about 1962, when it first realized that the animals' intelligence—and willingness to execute tasks for tasty fish rewards—could be of use in aquatic combat-related and reconnaissance operations. They perform underwater mine detection ("bomb sniffing"), equipment recovery, harbor guarding, and diver location. Dolphins can find enemy divers, then bump a device onto the back of their air tanks that sends up a buoy, signaling the intruders' presence to the dolphins' human handlers.

Other countries also use marine mammals in their military programs, including beluga whales—sweet-faced, playful animals that live in Arctic and sub-Arctic waters. They can be trained, but they don't enjoy warm water. Which makes them unlikely candidates for military service in temperate regions of the ocean.

In the spring of 2019, a "friendly" beluga approached some Norwegian fishermen. He had a harness strapped around him with a holder for a GoPro camera and made headlines as a possible "Russian spy."

The little white whale was named Hvaldimir by local voters in a poll—a name-pun that combined the Norwegian word for "whale" with the first name of the Russian autocrat Vladimir Putin. Hvaldimir became a celebrity in Norway, where he continued to reside until he disappeared from sight when monitoring of his movements was halted.

And the Russian navy apparently deployed dolphins in the Black Sea to protect its maritime base at Sevastopol in 2022, at the beginning of its invasion of Ukraine.

But such military programs are far from transparent: the US Navy's marine-mammal training effort was classified in 1967 and turned into a "black budget" program whose details are not publicly available.

Perhaps to allay public concerns about its treatment of these beloved animals, the navy's Space and Warfare Systems Command periodically releases reports on selected marine-mammal activities.

In 2017 it announced the death of a bottlenose dolphin who'd been euthanized due to ailments associated with old age. The animal's deployments had included the Persian Gulf War in 2003.

"Today, one of our eldest dolphins, a 46-year-old male named Makai, and one of our most celebrated veterans of the Iraq War, was peacefully and humanely put to rest," read the official statement.

Meanwhile the navy's war games in the ocean—which began around

a half-century ago and involve sonar technologies believed to hurt and
even kill marine mammals in large numbers—continue unabated.

OTHER ANIMALS AREN'T always grateful for our interventions on
their behalf. The language barrier makes it hard for us to convince them
that, at times, we have their best interests at heart.

I can drive to the northernmost tip of the Gulf of California in about
four hours from my house (as I did on my ill-fated honeymoon). In
this long finger of the Pacific that separates Baja California from the
Mexican mainland, the rarest cetacean of them all lives on the edge
of nonexistence.

As I write this, there are believed to be about ten vaquitas left.

These small, snub-nosed porpoises are being driven to extinction by
fishing for shrimp and for a large fish, also endangered, called the totoaba
whose swim bladders are prized commodities in Chinese folk medicine.
The illegal trade in totoaba bladders is run by criminal Mexican and Chinese cartels and has proved impossible to curb.

A desperate attempt to capture a vaquita for the purpose of perpetu-
ating the species ended in failure in 2017, when a hopeful team of biologists, aided by navy-trained dolphins, brought one back to an ocean pen
they'd painstakingly constructed.

But vaquitas are shy of humans, and the animal died in a matter of hours.

Probably of sheer fright.

IN THE 1980S a popular book was published called *The Secret Life
of Plants*—a predecessor, at least in its messaging, to the work on plant
sentience that would later be done by scientists like Simard and Gagliano
and Mancuso. Much of its content was soon exposed as pseudoscience
and fantasy. But it encouraged readers to talk to their houseplants, and
surely this did no harm.

Recently, over a game of cards and wine, I was exchanging stories with my old friends Karen and Mike who, like me, enjoy hiking and being in nature. We realized we all have the habit of casually talking to plants and animals: we stroll along and address them as we pass.

Hello, old man, we'll say to a saguaro cactus. Looking good, looking fat. Nice rains we had this summer, right? Or, Hey, you don't have to get mad, mama, we might say to a scolding bird near a nest. Wow, aren't you fabulous, we'll say to a blooming prickly pear.

This is normal to us.

But, said Karen, most people don't do it.

I guess they don't, I said.

SYMPATHY FOR THE beasts is often a matter of relative scale: when they're large enough for us to observe in detail, we embrace them more readily. So mammals, birds, amphibians, reptiles, and certain fish are relatable partly because of the visibility of their features, while insects and spiders and other tiny invertebrates are relegated to alienness. Maybe a primordial fear of the unseen kicks in.

Their size isn't the only attribute that alienates us from the bodies of invertebrates—we're uncomfortable with a multiplicity of legs and eyes, too. When a creature has more than four limbs or more than two eyes, unlike us, many experience a sense of repulsion. We may also feel an aversion to external skeletons made of chitin, extruding mouth parts, or the appearance of hairiness on membranes other than skin.

Still, size is a factor.

Small animals live in a different version of time, shifted to match their own scale. They tend to perceive an event as passing more slowly than we do. One study tested this by measuring how animals process visual information in the form of blinking light. When light blinks fast enough, humans perceive it as unwavering, a solid stream: we can't detect the high-frequency on-and-off switching. But tiny animals are able to perceive the blinking in far more subtle increments—the smaller an animal is, the more finely it perceives those intervals.

An event like a bullet flying through the air or a flyswatter descending, which for us is either completely imperceptible (the flight of the bullet) or a rapid blur of movement (the swatter), likely appears to them as occurring in slower motion.

This may explain why flies can be so hard to swat. Clutched in our giant's hand, the swatter descends toward them for what they perceive to be a long time. So they're able to move out of its path in what we see as an irritatingly speedy evasive maneuver.

The smaller creatures are, and the faster their metabolisms, the more slowly time may progress for them. To us, these small animals typically have short lifespans—in insects, counted in days or weeks instead of years. But to them, the lifespans may "feel"—though here I interject a subjective extrapolation—as long as ours do to us.

There are, no doubt, exceptions to the general rule that correlates size and metabolic rates to time perception, since only a few species have been tested. Also, a few small-bodied animals live much longer than people.

One quahog clam, known posthumously as Ming the Mollusk, apparently lived to be 507 before it was discovered off the coast of Iceland in 2006 (and in the process of verifying its remarkable age, of course, killed).

LARGE ANIMALS LIKE US are weak, compared to the very small. Gravity works against us, and much of our strength goes into bearing the weight of our own bodies.

Leafcutter ants can carry fifty times their own weight with their jaws, and the tiny necks of common American field ants, a 2014 study showed, can withstand pressures equal to five thousand times their weight.

The honor of being the smallest animal with bones may go to a species of anglerfish, though superlative assertions are always controversial. The male of *Photocorynus spiniceps*, an anglerfish that lives in the deep sea and was first reported in 2005 off the coast of the Philippines, can be as small as a quarter of an inch.

Anglerfish swim below about 3,000 feet, attract prey with a bioluminescent lure that looks like a headlamp, and then distend their jaws, and subsequently stomachs, in order to swallow prey that's sometimes as large as they are. Males spend part of their life cycles, or all of them in some species, attached to the larger bodies of the females—in the case of *spiniceps*, so much larger that, when you look at a picture of the two together, the males resemble a pimple on the females' backs.

Much of their body mass consists of testes. They're described, perhaps unfairly, as sexual parasites.

An anglerfish, with its lumpish body and ridiculously long, needle-sharp snaggleteeth, is hideous to the human eye—so ugly that it tests the proposition that aesthetics are subjective. Not for nothing did these ill-favored creatures evolve in the ocean's dark depths, surrounded by other nearly sightless beings.

Their glowing lures, mating habits, and life cycles down in that abysmal darkness are fascinating. But no matter how hard I stare at a picture of one, or a rare video captured by submersible—and despite the fish's long, ethereal tendrils that float around it in the water—I can't make myself see it as beautiful. Or even plain.

I challenge you to try this exercise.

One man has succeeded. Billed in an article in the *New York Times* as a foremost authority on anglerfish, Theodore Pietsch told the newspaper in 2019: "They're glorious, wonderful things that need our attention, and our protection."

Yes, I think, as I read his words. Yes. I agree. I love this man.

Because this man loves the anglerfish.

8

IN *HALF-EARTH*, THE late biologist E. O. Wilson—a winner of two Pulitzer Prizes and a special award from the Royal Swedish Academy that gives out Nobels—proposed we conserve half of the surface of the world for the wild.

Nothing less, he said, would be sufficient to ensure the survival of a richness of other life on the planet.

His challenge has been taken up by conservation groups like my own, which are calling for "50 by 2050"—the preservation of 50 percent of the global land and ocean in the next three decades. Both to save species from going extinct, since they need refugia to move into as the changing climate forces many to migrate, and to help curb climate change by preserving forests and other important biomes and leaving fossil fuels in the ground.

Along the way, the nearer-term goal is "30 by 2030," or "30×30."

Both of these benchmarks, at first, seem dauntingly ambitious. The Biden administration, in its first weeks, proudly proclaimed it was embracing 30×30.

But almost instantly, to ward off anticipated objections around the specters of land seizure and government overreach, this initiative became far more nebulous.

The language used to describe it was hastily switched: even its name lost the specificity of numbers, turning into "America the Beautiful," a watered-down campaign whose stated agenda lacks any direct reference to wildlife. And whose first priority is not the urgent protection of places but the careful production of an atlas.

IN *THE WORLD WITHOUT US*, Alan Weisman documented the recolonization by the wild of abandoned human places like Chernobyl, the demilitarized zone between North and South Korea, and an old-growth forest in Poland.

He imagined a scenario in which all human activity abruptly ceased and researched what the effects of that scenario would be, from the flooding tunnels of the New York subway system to the 441 nuclear plants across the world, which would melt down into hubs of radioactive poison within weeks.

For thousands of years our plastics and cast iron might remain to attest to our presence. Eventually these too would break down.

Only our radio waves, however fragmented and vestigial, could keep going out indefinitely. Snatches of word and song.

The last remnants of our presence may be language.

STARTING OUT AS a writer, my stories were comedies of manners or loose parodies. But the more I saw—the more I lived—the more evasive such mockeries began to seem to me.

Even now I don't like to write fiction that's without a trace of humor. Partly because it's hard to investigate human social behavior without an experience of breakdown—of the ridiculousness that crops up out of the tunnel vision of the self-absorbed. It's tough to resist, on the playing field of humanness, a harsh objectification of the un-self-aware.

And partly because I like to laugh as I write.

But it happens to me with increasing frequency, these days, that writing takes the form of prayer.

As in a dark booth, first comes a confession. And then an incantation. *There is a crack, a crack, in everything,* sang Leonard Cohen in "Anthem," my favorite of his songs. *That's how the light gets in.*

What could be more honest than a prayer? What's more heartfelt than begging?

The truest language of all is a plea for mercy.

You can pray to God, of course. But you can also pray to other people.

REMEMBERING TOO MUCH can be a hindrance.

There's a storehouse of personal guilts at the back of my mind filled with a motley assortment of choices, moments, and faces—mistakes I made and opportunities I missed. I visit this storehouse so rarely the lock's gotten rusty; inside the bare bulbs have burned out. Cobwebs hang between the statues of friends I allowed to fall away, small betrayals I perpetrated, failures of understanding. Blunt remarks I should have left unsaid. Even the killing of one small toad.

And a few injuries that I received in return, too. Hurts suffered and shelved away where they can do less harm.

So I've been grateful, on occasion, for forgetfulness as well as memory: it feels like liberation to be allowed, by the workings of my own mind, to walk away from that locked shed.

Forgetting is imperfect, but as selective and necessary as choosing to remember.

In the dementia or natural frailty and entropy of old age, many of us lose our hold on the choice. Confuse the now with then, the actual with the figment. Reach out to touch the familiar and find the tips of our fingers meeting nothing.

A moment can arrive when we try to remember the details of our own histories and discover them absent, empty spaces where meaning and referents are supposed to be. When this separation from remembering occurs, we start to fade into hollows—cease knowing ourselves, as well as those we hold dear. Shedding the pieces that made up the whole, lacking the delicate balance of forgetting and remembering that makes up coherent personhood, we move like phantoms over a shifting ground.

I've seen this happen in others and fear it for myself.

But another form of memory, stretching before and after us, also reaches its tendrils out under the firmament. Sometimes I wonder if, in the self-forgetting haze of mental decline, where our individual storylines become fragmentary and hold less sway, we may, in the odd moment, have a different access to that world beyond the self.

To the sensory present and our surroundings, after the past and the future recede. The longer epic of other animals and trees and grasses, of all that's green and turns the sun into breath and food.

Still visible and tangible in their forms and movements, even when our own backstory is gone. Immanent in these beings that, like us, could only arise, once and never again, from deep time.

The memory of the earth. Embodied.

I FIND MYSELF, at times, shunting away the specters of the future that hover in front of me. Enacting a deliberate forgetting of what's to come, much as I willfully forget the past when it suits me. Say, fearful visions of my girl and boy grown old and frail, lonely and frightened and unsheltered in the night. And, more and more, of the landscape they may be living in.

In the selfish ambition I clung to when I was young, I used to worry about my own welfare and persistence. But these days I worry about the persistence of everything I took for granted back then—the lasting splendor of my home.

Of all the homes.

If regret is the ghost of the past, for me, extinction is the ghost of the future.

Now my worry is less about leaving than of what will be left.

I hate the feeling.

And yet that turning outward of fear may be the only thing of true value that I've ever learned.

9
—

BEFORE WE HAD the tools for swift travel and recording, and for the wide dissemination of visual and auditory documents, we knew only the beasts and trees and plants that happened to live near us. Those who existed far away were little more than rumors, relayed in rare, hard-to-read manuscripts and fireside tales.

We had the colorful bestiaries of paper and parchment, inscribed on wood pulp and lambskin, and the informal bestiaries of our personal spheres—the smaller complement of beings we physically encountered.

Today we can see and hear multitudes. No volume could contain them all: the internet of animals is an endless archive. At the touch of a key we can bring their images into our field of view, hear their sounds, observe their movements and behaviors.

We're among the first generations to be able to know, not only by reporting but by the evidence of our eyes and ears, the awesome variety of the living—the multiplicity of its forms.

Among the first to command a view of the grandeur of what is.

And its precariousness.

THE *EARTHRISE* PHOTO from Apollo 8 was the first time people had seen the earth from outer space and is often cited as a watershed moment for human perception—a novel glimpse of the finiteness of our habitat. Of the isolation, and possibly uniqueness, of our warm blue-green sphere in the surrounding dark and cold.

Sometimes, when the *Earthrise* picture is reshown, it introduces the idea of a dawning of environmental consciousness. In the United States and beyond.

What dawned? Was there a shock of recognition followed by reckoning? Was the flurry of new environmental laws passed in the early 1970s, with their many efforts to preserve life-support systems, one echo of that witnessing?

Was it only our words that changed?

Those laws—the words of reckoning—have made a difference.

But the part about love is still only a whisper.

"THE LOVE THAT dare not speak its name," wrote an Englishman named Lord Alfred Douglas in 1894.

He was referring to romantic and sexual love between men, which was then a crime in England. Up until 1861, it had been punishable by hanging.

Whatever the flaws and tragedies of language, whatever the pitfalls of disclosure and definition, we have to speak our love to make it known.

And our loss. We have to mourn each disappearance. No death is deeper than an extinction.

In our rush to get past the grief of death, we also rush past the exuberance of being alive.

IN LONELY HOURS I'm haunted by the certainty that the errors we're making in the dominion of being, across the sweep of existence, aren't recoverable. That we're losing what can never be replaced.

I think of the line between desperation and despair, those two words with the same root but such a different feel. Of how the first can drive us and the second defeat us.

The protection of a lifeform requires a dedication of effort and resources, for sure. But while the curbing of global climate change depends on a mass mobilization, the prevention of an extinction can occur on a small scale. Sometimes on a span of only a few acres, other times across urban patchworks or regions.

Some of the other kinds can likely only be saved by the same carbon-reduction measures that will save our own—those of the melting Arctic, those of the coral reefs—but there are countless others we can preserve through more direct and local means. At times as simple as deciding not to build a gas station or resort in their last home.

In many cases a creature's continued presence in the world may be secured without much pain or sacrifice at all—an act of care, a decision. The extinction of other lifeforms is preventable.

One by one and two by two, as the story tells us the beasts were ushered into the Ark, they can be ushered in again.

Remember the future, I have to tell myself, when desperation shades into despair. Remember not only your fear but your hope—remember the possibilities.

Of a peaceful village or a green countryside. A city on a hill. A glowing place with soft shadows.

Of the fellowship of strangers.

THE GARDEN OF EDEN tale tells us this: that the eating of the forbidden fruit, the fruit of the tree of knowledge of good and evil, was a sin. It was a sin because it went against the single rule the Creator had given to his people. And when we disobeyed that rule and chose knowledge, we were severed from the rest of the beasts.

The Creator, being omniscient, would have known this as he knew all things—that our choice of knowledge would remove us from the realm of the others he had also created.

That this departure, this severance from the other animals, would become our original sin.

And that, over time, the very nature of that sin would be obscured from our sight.

It was the choosing of knowledge that banished us from our union with the others, in the story of Eden.

But lately our knowledge has brought us closer to them again. We've built equipment that lets us see the earth from outside it, allows us to explore the far corners of the lands and seas. Found ways to see and hear the others, as well as our own kind, from almost anywhere—to cast waves into the ocean that tell us the shapes and positions of whales and schools of fish, into the air to describe the patterns of storms and ice and fire.

Into the universe to understand celestial objects we couldn't reach in a thousand lifetimes.

Those ways might be seen as a miracle of creation—even, to the faithful, as a permission or dispensation from on high. An act of divine clemency: the chance of an atonement for all the sins of omission and commission our kind has committed against the rest.

With our far-seeing, we've afforded ourselves the opportunity of using our ability to know—the shimmering privilege that, through story and stubborn pride, has held us separate from the others for so long—to also be wise.

And preserve the wonders we still have.

EVERY LIFE IS a jumble of event, swells of drama and stretches of sameness. Some lend themselves to repetition, with bright, public flashes of victory and defeat, scandal and conflict, while others unspool along private paths.

But none is without story, and no story is without fascination. Held up to the light, each life glitters with the intrigues and crises of selfhood and community. Even in darkness, unseen, a living thing breathes with its own particular glory. Its own rhythm of existence, never exactly the same as the next.

An extraordinary experience of being, even within a so-called ordinary life.

The world of subjectivity beyond the human is also vested with that charismatic gleam: the light of other beings. Who offer us discoveries that surpass our understanding. Encounters with the new and with newness itself—the novelty we need to nourish our minds and our moods, to invest our experience of living with thrill and uplift and euphoria.

With the neural and existential romance of the not-yet-known.

The others are the manifested, diverse brilliance of the force that animates us all. We can use the language of mysticism or religion or science to insult or exalt them, but our words remain shadows and light. Playing over the surface of things and furnishing us, as we abide on that surface, with a complex illusion of meaning.

The truths of sentience persist beyond and beside the symbols we've made, in spaces language can reach for but never touch.

So that humility before nature, as well as what we hold to be divine, is the only wise course left.

The workings of life across time preexisted our words and their illusions and will outlast them by eons—into the swelling and then the dwindling of the sun. And possibly beyond, with the rise and fall of trillions of other stars.

Astonishing and irreducible, those works imbue the universe with feeling and with warmth.

The sharp grief and delectation of presence and mortality, the possibility of joy.

IN THE HIGHEST mountain reaches I can drive to easily from my home, ponderosa pines are the dominant trees. They give off a smell like sun-warmed caramel. The forests they form open up into airy spaces, carpeted with brown needles that crunch pleasantly underfoot as you walk.

A curious scent from the trees envelops you—almost of longing. Almost of nostalgia.

When the wind moves the branches, and you stand still to listen, the sound it makes is a *hush*.

A soughing sigh that dispels and elevates silence.

And feels like company.

10

IT WAS A sifting sand that blew through the cracks in our doors and windows and piled up in the rooms of our houses: the sedimentation of habit.

We never intended it to be this way, we never planned it, but somehow we became a people of entitlement—to pleasure, to comfort, and to the worship not of qualities and character but of objects. False idols, they used to be called.

Honor and sacrifice have receded, to be invoked only in selective, sanctimonious reference to military personnel or emergency first responders. Never to the many others among us who give up a life of ease to work in service to the rest—teachers, librarians, linemen, those who toil for low wages in sanitation or sewage, at the post office or in grueling jobs on the farms and in the factories that bring us our food.

I'VE ALWAYS BEEN a lazy dresser, preferring not to have to think too much about the clothes I put on. So I often cycle through hastily adopted uniforms, usually in shades of moss green and black, and typically decline to change up the uniform for work obligations. For a few months' time my uniform of choice was camo pants in a loose cargo style, to hold my phone and other necessary objects without my having to lug around a purse, and chunky black boots to ward off the diamondback rattlesnakes who are so abundant in my yard.

Once, at the lobby level of a Miami hotel where I was staying briefly to promote a book, a young tourist couple got into the elevator with me.

If I had to guess, I'd say they were honeymooners. A few sheets to the wind.

As was I, honestly.

She was wearing a pink sheath minidress and balanced on high, tippy heels; he was glowing with a fresh Florida tan.

They were giggling and kissing when they came through the doors but quickly sobered at the sight of me in my camo pants and chunky black boots.

"Well. Thank you for your service," she said solemnly, as they got out.

Silently I inclined my head.

BUT SOME FORMS of duty, even as the sacred and the communal recede, are still held by most of us to be sacrosanct.

And chief among them, performed without pay or often even gratitude—out of sheer instinct—is the devotion of parenthood.

ONE OF THE things I found most remarkable, as a new mother, was the way parents of young children acted with each other.

As a childless person in my twenties, living in LA and New York, I was used to the wariness of strangers. They might be polite, but there was always a guardedness to first meetings. Especially in public places, where a lone stranger might be anyone—might even present a threat.

But as soon as I had a small child and took her with me to those same

public places—a park, a city square, a playground, a store or restaurant—
the guard of others was let down.

Especially if they, too, had a child in tow.

With a child attached, I no longer presented a possible threat. With a
child attached there was a different social understanding: like those other
parents, I existed in a state of exposure my child conferred on me. Like
them, I had to be protective.

Suddenly, in our duty of protection, we found ourselves in community. Sometimes the conversations were irritating or trivial, for sure—
sometimes a parent's attachment to his or her progeny might even strike
us as cloying—but still, on the subject of our children and our parenthood, we could confide in each other.

To me it doesn't seem like such a stretch for us to see our parenthood—
that sheltering, that deep, abiding love we know to be our legacy and
honor—as a duty of care that reaches beyond the present well-being of
our children into their far prospects. Beyond the horizon of the narrow
and personal into the land beyond.

The future of our children is also the future of the others. Not a life
on a private island, holed up against the rising winds and seas, but in a
sprawling commonwealth of need.

What if we said: our parenthood is not the lonely consecration of our
own, of what has emerged from us, but also of the many they depend on?
What if we turned, in a dawning instant, and saw ourselves for what we
are—the parents of the world to come?

Without the mysterious and the other and the wild, without the
many gifts they give us of sustenance and cohesion and possibility, those
who come later will inherit a poor kingdom. Even if our grandchildren
or great-grandchildren can manage to eke out a living in the bareness of
what remains, they'll be moving through time as orphans.

Orphaned by us, after we're gone, in our failures of foresight and
empathy. Orphaned as a kind, with fewer and fewer of the others still
alive to keep them company.

No ancient cousins, no far-flung families in the forests or ocean or
skies to hold the children of our children safe beneath their wings.

THE WORD *SPIRIT* comes from words meaning "breath," while the word *soul*, in some etymologies, is said to have come from the Proto-Germanic word for "sea." Coming from, or belonging to, the sea.

Soul and spirit are the stuff of water and air. Vast and amorphous bodies, forces of powerful tides and winds—the life-giving media of the earth.

What if the spirit and the soul we have are shared? What if they exist, like the ocean and the atmosphere, in a great pool? As a collective we already always belong to, into which we offer particles of ourselves?

This is a mystical projection, the notion of our continuity with the substances of the universe, but also attested to by aspects of physical life. Emerging more and more into our awareness.

How we share the atoms we breathe with both our ancestors and our descendants. And with the other forms that live.

How the hive minds of bees allow them to act as though a single will directs their movements. The nest-building of ants, the flocking of birds, the herding of ungulates, the schooling of fish and krill.

Maybe the individuation of the soul, its division and separation into personal property, is like the imprisonment of time in a grid.

GILDED BY WISHFULNESS, without specific words to make it real, hope remains formless. A swell of feeling, an affect forever tilted toward the tomorrow of what could, but might not ever, be. Like faith, it has the tinge of unrequited love, since the devout believe themselves beloved by God even through hardship and abandonment—even in the face of strong evidence that they have been forsaken.

Faith consists of a loyalty beyond reason, against which reason is useless.

Hope too hovers outside strict rationality. We can hope for the others and hope for ourselves, and certainly the abandonment of hope would lay us flat. Scholars who study hope have shown that certain forms may be defeatist while others are necessary for action. But by itself, in the absence of a striving to define and realize its objects, it can easily be reduced to surrender.

We can argue that the beasts and the green have a *right* to survive or that we have a *right* to their sustainment. We've made such assertions of ethics and inherent rights—such as the right to life, liberty, and the pursuit of happiness—on our own behalf.

And in the domain of the others, also, in the fullness of time, such arguments might hold sway.

But someday isn't soon enough.

And honestly, we shouldn't have to argue. If we can pause in the clamor of story, assuming the stillness that allows us to see, we know it as we know our children are good. And need us.

All that we really have to know is the need of all the young— the young beasts and the seedlings, along with the young we get to call our own.

It's the young, these days, who ask us for mercy and wait for us to answer. Ask that we act in their names instead of our own. Ask that we tell ourselves a better story than the one about winning and losing, about conquering and subsuming. A story that embraces the past along with the future, the powerless and speechless along with the loud and the blustering.

Even a story, say, that invites us not to want to be better than. But to want to be good.

MAYBE WE CAN take the path through the woods, which leads back to a curving world. Maybe we can move toward a dream of the wild and the real, past the boxes that hold them at bay.

Maybe we can step through the frames we've built all around. Through the doors and windows into the boundless air. Into the struggle that's called for—the only grace that can save.

A hope made real by covenant. By a story, a science, and a law of kindness.

Because even paradise has rules.

I LIKE TO be by myself, to write and to read and to walk, but only when I know I can go home afterward and be with my family again. Or out with my friends.

Most of us savor our personal solitude, which brings us breathing room and a blissful quiet.

As long as we can choose it.

In prison, where interaction between inmates is dangerous and often ugly, solitary confinement is still among the cruelest and most wretched punishments we can dole out. Its cells keep prisoners in isolation—away from their fellow convicts—but also tend to deny them the simple consolation of a window.

Access to the changing light of days, a glimpse of the world outside.

The saving of our descendants from a dreary solitariness of being is the single task, among so many stretching before us, that can only be performed *now*. In the rushing time of our too-short lives.

It commands us to shelter them: the meek and the ferocious, the lovely, the monstrous, the ragged and serene. Those that are known to us and those still to be discovered, but every single one of them our longtime companions.

The ones whose flocks swoop and shift in changing formations far above our heads as the blue turns violet, swim or drift through the ocean, thunder in herds over grasslands and tundra, lumber through the forests. The ones that make up the seas themselves, the plains, the jungles, and the mountainsides.

Then—even if history does turn out to be, for our kind, a line and not a circle—at the end it will be as it was in the beginning.

We will be able to gaze upon the things that grow, the creeping things, the flying things. The things that swim, the plodding creatures of the field. All those that we gave names and kept beside us.

And behold the shining faces of the infinite. To some, the face of God.

For the promised land was given to us long ago.

Look! Look.

Heaven was here the whole time.

And we were never meant to be alone.

ACKNOWLEDGMENTS

This book was a collective effort and I relied on other readers and writers for both criticism and facts; any mistakes and flaws belong only to me.

Tom Mayer, my excellent editor at Norton, did a delicate balancing act reordering passages and envisioning rhythm and shape. I'm in debt to my dear friends Jenny Offill, Randolph Heard, and Richard Nash for their time and clear insights. And, always, to Maria Massie, my thoughtful agent on every book since the second.

I thank Noah Greenwald, my first mentor at the Center for Biological Diversity, who let me be his thirty-year-old data-entry intern in 1999 despite my dubious résumé and later screened this manuscript for errors of natural history. I thank several other coworkers at the Center for their assistance: Hannah Connor on slaughterhouses; Bill Snape on Citizens United and judicial supremacy, though much of it ended up on the cutting-room floor; Mike Stark for his expertise on short-faced bears, similarly cut; Nate Donley for resources on 2,4-d; and Kierán Suckling for his magnanimity in being a subject, his biodiversity fact-checking, and his language on philosophers. I thank Kathy Meyer for reviewing material on laws covering animal cruelty.

I'm grateful to my mother, Saralaine Millet, for her patience and memory and love of her children, and to my late father, Nicholas Millet, for his devotion to animal stories and his romantic heart. I thank my uncle Chop Evans for his good humor and my aunt Brenda Evans for her record-sharing; my sister and brother, Mandy and Josh Millet, for being so good; and my cousins Ben and Nick Edlund for their help on deceased toads and our personal past. I thank the friends whose input on this has been lost as the text got whittled down—Roderick Cameron, Kim Miller, Karen Mockler, Kate Bernheimer, David Hancocks, Tom Pringle—but whose weighing in is appreciated.

I thank Elizabeth Riley, my publicist and one of my favorite people, for her intelligence and energy. I thank Steve Colca in marketing, Nneoma Amadi-obi in editorial, Ingsu Liu for art direction, David High for jacket design, Eve Sanoussi for her intrepid research, and Anna Oler and Don Rifkin, as well as several fearless book champions in sales, Meg Sherman, Steven Pace, Karen Rice, Sharon Gamboa, and Mike Harrigan. I thank Dan Christiaens, Joe Murphy, Suzette Ciancio, Dave Mallman, Ashanti White-Wallace, Abby Fennewald, and Golda Rademacher. Amy Robbins, my copyeditor on several books now, converts my words out of stubborn AP style and catches embarrassing errors.

On the home front I thank my partner, Aaron Young, for his work and love, and my children Nola and Silas.